UNIVERSITY OF NORTH CAROLINA
STUDIES IN THE ROMANCE LANGUAGES AND LITERATURES
Number 112

THE SIGNIFICANCE OF DIDEROT'S
ESSAI SUR LE MÉRITE ET LA VERTU

THE SIGNIFICANCE OF DIDEROT'S
ESSAI SUR LE MÉRITE ET LA VERTU

BY
GORDON B. WALTERS, JR.

CHAPEL HILL
THE UNIVERSITY OF NORTH CAROLINA PRESS

depósito legal: v. 4.875 - 1971

artes gráficas soler, s. a. — jávea, 28 — valencia (8) — 1971

TABLE OF CONTENTS

	Pages
CHAPTER ONE: THE *ESSAI* AND THE *INQUIRY*: HOW THEY DIFFER ...	17
I. *Theism, Deism, and Atheism.*	
1. The Distinction Between Theism and Deism	17
2. The Question of Universal Order	20
3. Atheism and Free-Thought	30
II. *Religious Fanaticism*	35
III. *Social and Political Abuses*	60
IV. *Virtue*	71
1. Virtue and Happiness	72
2. The Question of Objective Values	78
3. The Moral Sense: "cœur," "sentiment intérieur," "conscience"	84
4. Virtue and The Passions	88
5. Virtue and Self-Interest	92
CHAPTER TWO: THE STYLE OF THE *ESSAI*	97
CONCLUSION	115

for SHARON

To my teachers — James Doolittle, Jean Parrish, and Herbert Dieckmann — who have inspired in me an interest in French literature of the eighteenth century I offer my thanks; to Richard Frautschi of Pennsylvania State University I am indebted for his suggestions and help in preparing this study for publication.

PREFACE

There is no need to insist here upon the importance of Diderot's 1745 translation of Shaftesbury's *An Inquiry Concerning Virtue or Merit* as a document which enables us to understand better the evolution of Diderot's thought and artistic skill. The *Essai sur le mérite et la vertu,* because the translator very frequently sees fit to significantly modify the original, constitutes the first work of Diderot in which we can see something that really belongs to him.

The *Essai* was not of course Diderot's first effort at translating from the English. His rendition of Temple Stanyan's *Grecian History* appeared in three volumes in 1739, and, in the opinion of Arthur Wilson, "If one be content to ask no more of a translation than that it be accurate and faithful, a comparison of the original and of th French version shows that Diderot was quite a skillful translator." [1] Hence, in fact, the translation of Stanyan is much less significant for Diderot students than the *Essai:* "Si de ce bon livre Diderot retiendra des exemples et des anecdotes dont il illustrera plus tard ses raisonnements, nous ne saurions vraiment rien tirer de là, qui nous renseigne sur ce que pense le philosophe à l'époque où il traduit l'histoire anglaise." [2]

On the other hand, Professor Wilson states that "There is a great deal of the characteristic Diderot in the *Essai:* the mischievous and pointed placing of footnotes where Shaftesbury's implicit heterodoxy was most apparent; the lengthy quotation from skeptical

---

[1] Arthur M. Wilson, *Diderot: The Testing Years, 1713-1759,* New York, 1959, p. 50. For a more detailed analysis of Diderot's first effort at translating from the English see W. Folkierski, "L'Anglais de Diderot," *Revue de Littérature comparée,* avril-juin 1960, 226-244.

[2] Pierre Hermand, *Les Idées morales de Diderot,* Paris, 1923, p. 50.

authors like Montaigne or extremely pagan ancients like Petronius; the use of concepts, that, like leitmotives, occur in Diderot's later writings...; the extremely personal approach to the reader, even in works of philosophy..." (Wilson, *op. cit.*, pp. 51-52). The influence of Shaftesbury upon Diderot is perceptible for many years, and particularly, as many commentators have shown, in his first "philosophical" works. Paolo Casini, for example, finds something of Shaftesbury even in Diderot's early atheistic materialism: "Diderot si manterrà sempre fedele alla concezione della natura come un tutto organico, vivente, eternamente operante in infinite guise, animato da un perpetuo dinamismo, appresa dalle *Characteristicks*." [3]

Still, if critics of Diderot agree that his *Essai* provides insight into his early thought, except for Martin Löpelmann's study, *Der Junge Diderot* [4] (Part II, Chapter I), there has been no genuinely serious examination of the translation itself, or of the ways in which Diderot *traducteur* alters the original text and why he does so. Pierre Hermand admits that only the notes of the *Essai* interest him: "On ne peut ... vraiment tirer du texte même aucune conclusion touchant les idées du traducteur; car il serait d'une mauvaise méthode d'admettre que Diderot fit siennes toutes les idées de l'auteur qu'il présente au public français" (Hermand, *op. cit.*, p. 53). Cru, Pommier, Venturi, Wilson, Casini [5] — most of those writers who have concentrated on Diderot's "formative years" — affirm that the translation is not always faithful, [6] but

---

[3] Paolo Casini, "Diderot e Shaftesbury," *Giornale critico della filosofia italiana*, XXXIX (XIV), 1960, p. 269.

[4] Martin Löpelmann, *Der Junge Diderot*, Berlin, 1934, Part II, Chapter I.

[5] R. L. Cru, *Diderot and English Thought*, New York, 1913; Jean Pommier, *Diderot avant Vincennes*, Paris, 1939; Franco Venturi, *La Jeunesse de Diderot*, Paris, 1939.

[6] For example, Casini: "La traduzione è ... libera, ma sostanzialmente vicina all'originale" (*op. cit.*, p. 254); René Legros, in "Diderot et Shaftesbury," *Modern Language Review*, 1924, 189: "[Diderot] a traduit le texte librement"; Wilson (*op. cit.*, p. 50) calls the translation "more a paraphrase than a translation"; Pommier (*op. cit.*, p. 60): "Cette prétendue traduction...."; and, finally, Dorothy B. Schlegel, *Shaftesbury and The French Deists*, Chapel Hill, N. C., 1956, p. 45: "In spite of Diderot's avowal of comparative independance of the original of his translation, his work is as close a rendition of Shaftesbury's text as the French language and his systematic mind would permit."

little attention is given to the reasons *why* this is the case. Many students [7] of Diderot conclude, without really showing what they mean, that the interpolations on Shaftesbury's text embody a "personal" approach. Some commentators take Diderot at his word and assume that most of the footnotes serve to soften the blow of some of Shaftesbury's bolder assertions. Franco Venturi has conscientiously traced some of the textual sources of Diderot's notes, [8] but he has rarely paused to interpret in detail the significance of their content and context, and he has given no real attention to the French rendering of the English text itself. Paolo Casini devotes the greater part of his article "Diderot e Shaftesbury" to an assessment of the influence of the English thinker upon the works which follow the *Essai* rather than to problems which relate to the translation itself; similarly, he has little to say of the character of the translation in his book, *Diderot "Philosophe"* (Bari, Laterza, 1962; "La traduzione dell' 'Inquiry concerning Virtue, or Merit,'" p. 53 f.).

The present study consists of an analysis of both the translation of Shaftesbury's text and Diderot's footnotes (one might indeed call them "pensées philosophiques," for Diderot thinks of them as "réflexions") [9] in order to see what of Shaftesbury Diderot modifies and what new material Diderot adds to Shaftesbury's argument; finally we will examine the nature of the stylistic changes wrought by Diderot the translator.

As the reader will learn from my "Table of Contents," the material wherein Diderot's modification of the original is most remarkable I have arranged according to subject headings. I have not done this gratuitously: in the main, Diderot's translation deviates from the original when he disagrees with Shaftesbury or when he wishes to emphasize a point made by the Englishman.

---

[7] See again, for example, Wilson, *op. cit.*, p. 51, and Casini, *op. cit.*, p. 254.

[8] *La Jeunesse*, pp. 342-357.

[9] Diderot, *Essai sur le mérite et la vertu*, in *Œuvres*, ed. Assézat-Tourneux, 1876, I, 16. All subsequent references are to this edition. All references to Shaftesbury's works are to *The Characteristics*, in the widely available edition by J. M. Robertson (London, 1900), although I have as well consulted a three-volume edition of 1723, which Diderot may well have used. References to the *Inquiry* are to Robertson, I, 234-338.

In effect, the arrangement of our material according to "themes," e.g., theism, deism, and atheism; religious fanaticism; social and political questions, suggests itself, since these are the issues which apparently so interested Diderot at the time he undertook the work on the *Inquiry* that he was stimulated to insert his own opinions into the "translation."

While Diderot's translation of Shaftesbury is then commentary of a sort, the translator's notes constitute a more *direct* commentary on the ideas presented in the body of the essay. Moreover, we cannot positively claim that the notes were written (in entirety or in part) at the same time as the translation. For these reasons it has seemed advisable to separate our study of textual material from that of Diderot's notes. In both Chapter I and Chapter II therefore, evidence from the text of the *Essai* is considered first in each topic case, followed by evidence from Diderot's notes, which in fact most often broadens the nature of the material which he has inserted into "Shaftesbury's" text.

In my citations of both Shaftesbury and Diderot, the italics are mine unless otherwise noted.

CHAPTER I

THE *ESSAI* AND THE *INQUIRY*: HOW THEY DIFFER

I. THEISM, DEISM, AND ATHEISM

1. *The Distinction Between Theism and Deism*

A. The *Discours préliminaire* and Textual Modifications.

In the *Discours préliminaire* of his *Essai* Diderot makes clear the fact that he does not wish that the translator of the *Inquiry* be labelled an apologist of deism, for he draws a sharp distinction between deism and theism upon which Shaftesbury himself does not insist.[1] On the pretext of defending Shaftesbury against the charge that he advocates a disbelief in revelation, Diderot cites the following passage from *The Moralists*:

> For as averse as I am to the cause of theism, or name of Deist, when taken in a sense exclusive of revelation, I consider still that in strictness the root of all is theism, and that to be a settled Christian, it is necessary to be first of all a good theist; *for theism can only be opposed to polytheism or atheism.* Nor have I patience to hear the name of *Deist* (the highest of all names) decried, and set in opposition to Christianity. "As if our religion was a kind of magic, which depended not on the belief of a single supreme Being. Or as if the firm and rational

---

[1] Dorothy B. Schlegel (*Shaftesbury and The French Deists*, University of North Carolina Studies in Comparative Literature, no. 15, Chapel Hill, N. C., 1956; p. 47 f.) has seen that Diderot fabricates the distinction, and she has indicated some of the instances in which he does so.

belief of such a Being on philosophical grounds was an improper qualification for believing anything further." Excellent presumption for those who naturally incline to the disbelief of revelation, or who through vanity affect a freedom of this kind! (*Moralists*, 19)

But Diderot makes two important modifications in *his* quotation of the original. He first omits the phrase "for theism can only be opposed to polytheism or atheism," an omission which would demonstrate that he wishes to emphasize a strong opposition as well between theism and *deism*. Secondly, he replaces the word "Deist" with "Theist," and thus focuses the reader's attention on a close relationship between *theism* and Christianity (*Essai*, 14). In the paragraph previous to his citation of Shaftesbury, Diderot had already given evidence of deliberately misrepresenting Shaftesbury's attitude toward deism: "En anglais, le mot de *theist* désigne indistinctement *déiste* et *théiste*" (Diderot's italics), which indeed appears to be true, as far as Shaftesbury is concerned; but it is not the case that this lack of distinction is for Shafesbury a "Confusion odieuse" — "contre laquelle se récrie M.... S...., qui n'a pu supporter qu'on prostituât à une troupe d'impies le nom de *théistes*, le plus auguste de tous les noms" (*Essai*, 13; Diderot's italics). Deists are elsewhere treated harshly by Diderot, for he groups them with other "impies" — atheists, sociniens, and spinozists (*Essai*, 12). He reiterates later the contrast between deism and theism where Shaftesbury does not do so: "*Le déisme*, le théisme, l'athéisme, et même le démonisme, n'ont aucune action immédiate et directe relativement à la distinction morale de la droiture et de l'injustice..." (*Essai*, 44; see *Inquiry*, 241).

Diderot thus goes to some lengths in the *Discours préliminaire* to show that Shaftesbury's philosophy is in no way antipathetic to revelation: he cites (p. 15) a passage from *Miscellaneous Reflections* (see Robertson, II, 352) in which Shaftesbury declares that he is, for all practical purposes, "Conformist to the lawful church," and concludes that "Je ne conçois pas comment, après des protestations aussi solennelles d'une entière soumission de cœur et d'esprit aux mystères sacrés de la religion, il s'est trouvé quelqu'un assez injuste pour compter M... S... au nombre des *Asgil*, des *Tindal*, et des *Toland*" (Diderot's italics).

B. Additions

In a note to the passage "To believe therefore that everything is governed, ordered, or regulated for the best, by a designing principle or mind, necessarily good and permanent, is to be a perfect Theist" (*Inquiry*, 240), Diderot cautions "Gardez-vous bien de confondre ce mot [theist] avec celui de déiste" (*Essai*, 21 note; Diderot's italics). Note 1, page 22 presents the material found on pages 241-42 of the *Inquiry;* Diderot lists the various forms of religious belief, as does Shaftesbury; but Diderot, unlike Shaftesbury, mentions both theism *and* deism:

1. Theism [may be mixed] with Daemonism; 2. Daemonism with Polytheism; 3. Theism with Atheism.... (*Inquiry*, 241)	Le théisme [peut se mélanger] avec le démonisme. Le démonisme avec le polythéisme. Le déisme avec l'athéisme....

Diderot indicates here again that theism and deism are not identical; but what is more, he suggests that theism is antithetical to atheism while deism may be similar to atheism in certain respects. It is quite apparent, in the footnote-additions as well as in the modifications made within the text itself, that Diderot is intent upon opposing deism and theism, and that he does so on the basis of the relationship of theism and deism to *revealed* religion. As we have seen, deists are criticized in the *Discours préliminaire* on the grounds that they are "ennemis de toute révélation" (*Essai*, 13); the antithesis is rendered fully explicit when we are told in note 1, page 60 that theists are "près d'admettre" revelation. Yet despite this defense of theism as sympathetic to revelation, Diderot gives scant attention in what he adds to the *Inquiry* to the importance and efficacy of revealed religion, and we must assume that he presents Shaftesbury as a theist and the *Inquiry* as a theistic tract in the interest of experiency and safety. [2]

---

[2] It is to be further noted, of course, that the distinction between deism and theism is no longer maintained in the *Pensées philosophiques* of 1746: indeed, Shaftesbury, it seems, is now a *deist* (see *pensée* XIII). The deist is no longer "impie," but one who accepts the existence of God, the immortality of the soul, "et ses suites" (XXIII). However, explicit mention of

2. The Question of Universal Order

A. Textual modifications.

Shaftesbury's confident vision of universal order is of course fundamental to his "theism," but Diderot's hesitancy in wholeheartedly concurring with Shaftesbury's beliefs is manifested in several instances of modification of Shaftesbury's argument. The first example of a disagreement is to be found quite early in the *Essai:*

There are few who think always consistently, or according to one certain hypothesis, upon any subject so abstruse and intricate as the cause of all things, and the economy or government of the universe. For 'tis evident in the case of the most devout people, even by their own confession, that there are times when their faith can hardly support them in the belief of a supreme Wisdom, and that they are often tempted to judge disadvantageously of a providence and just administration in the whole. (*Inquiry*, 241)	Il y a peu de personnes qui aient été en tout temps invariablement attachés à la même hypothèse sur un sujet aussi profond que la cause universelle des êtres et l'économie générale du monde: de l'aveu même des personnes les plus religieuses, toute leur foi leur suffit à peine, en certains moments, pour les soutenir dans la conviction d'une intelligence suprême; il est des conjonctures où, frappés des *défauts apparents de l'administration de l'univers,* elles sont *violemment* tentées de juger désavantageusement de la Province. (*Essai*, 21-22)

More serious exception is evident at the beginning of Part II:

> When we reflect on any ordinary frame or constitution either of Art or Nature, and consider how hard it is to give the least account of a particular part without a competent knowledge of the whole, we need not wonder to find ourselves at a loss in many things relating to the constitution and frame of Nature herself. For to what end

---

the deist's belief in revelation is nowhere to be found in the *Pensées philosophiques.*

in Nature many things, even whole species of creatures, refer, or to what purpose they serve, will be hard for any one justly to determine; but to what end the many proportions and various shapes of parts in many creatures actually serve, we are able, by the help of study and observation, to demonstrate with great exactness. (*Inquiry*, 243)

Shaftesbury declares that there are many phenomena in Nature that are difficult for us to understand, but nevertheless that there are many cases in which we can precisely demonstrate the purpose of biological organization. Diderot, on the other hand, reverses Shaftesbury's point and pays greater heed to our weaknesses.

Lorsque je tourne les yeux sur les ouvrages d'un artiste, ou sur quelque production ordinaire de la nature, et que je sens en moi-même combien il est difficile de parler avec exactitude des *parties*, sans une connaissance profonde du *tout*, je ne suis point étonné de notre insuffisance dans les recherches qui concernent le monde, le chef-d'œuvre de la nature. Cependant, à force d'observations et d'étude, à force de combiner les proportions et les formes dont la plupart des créatures qui nous environnent sont revêtues, nous sommes parvenus à déterminer quelques-uns de leurs usages. Mais quelle est la fin de ces créatures en particulier? En général même, à quoi sert l'espèce entière de quelques-unes d'entre elles? C'est ce que nous ne connaîtrons peut-être jamais. (*Essai*, 23; Diderot's emphasis)

"Je ne suis point étonné de notre *insuffisance* dans les recherches..." The allusion to "les recherches" further suggests that Diderot conceives an active *investigation* which is not fully achieving its ends. Diderot then replaces Shaftesbury's assured statement (.... to what end the many proportions and various shapes of parts in many creatures actually serve, we are able ... to demonstrate with great exactness") with one of much greater modesty: "Cependant, à force d'observations et d'étude, à force de combiner les proportions et les formes dont la plupart des créatures qui nous environnent sont revêtues, nous sommes parvenus à déterminer *quelques-uns de leurs usages*." But finally, Diderot concludes *his* paragraph with a confession of ignorance and even despair: ".... C'est ce que nous connaîtrons peut-être *jamais*."

B. Additions

To be sure, in note 1, page 62, Diderot relates the ecstasy experienced by the "philosophe" who contemplates the vastness of Creation: "A mesure que l'univers s'étend aux yeux d'un philosophe, tout ce qui l'environne se rapetisse. La terre s'évanouit sous ses pieds. Lui-même, que devient-il? Cependant il ressent un doux frémissement dans cette contemplation qui l'anéantit; après s'être vu noyé, pour ainsi dire, et perdu dans l'immensité des êtres, il éprouve une satisfaction secrète à se retrouver sous les yeux de la Divinité." [3] Other additions do not however reflect the enthusiasm represented in this case. In the four notes to be cited here, Diderot expresses reservations about universal order which are based again, as they were in the textual modifications which we have already examined, upon the question of *demonstration* or upon the extent to which order is apparent in what we see about us. Diderot admits, in note 1, page 49, that the "miracles de la nature" are not understood or even appreciated by all of us.

> Les miracles de la nature sont exposés à nos yeux, longtemps avant que nous ayons assez de raison pour en être éclairés. Si nous arrivions dans ce monde avec cette raison que nous portâmes dans la salle de l'Opéra, la première

---

[3] This note is undoubtedly inspired in part by the following oration of Theocles in *The Moralists* (Robertson, II, 89):

> ....O mighty Nature! wise substitute of Providence! impowered creatress! Or thou impowering Deity, supreme creator! Thee I invoke and thee alone adore. To thee this solitude, this place, these rural meditations are alone sacred; whilst thus inspired with harmony of thought, though unconfined by words, and in loose numbers, I sing of Nature's order in created beings, and celebrate the beauties which resolve in thee, the source and principle of all beauty and perfection.
> Thy being is boundless, unsearchable, impenetrable. In thy immensity all thought is lost, fancy gives over its flight, and wearied imagination spends itself in vain, finding no coast nor limit of this ocean, nor, in the widest tract through which it soars, one point yet nearer the circumference than the first centre whence it parted. Thus having oft essayed, thus sallied forth into the wide expanse, when I return again within mvself, struck with the sense of this so narrow being and of the true fulness of that immense one, I dare no more behold the amazing depths nor sound the abyss of Deity.

> fois que nous y entrâmes, et si la toile se levait brusquement, frappés de la grandeur, de la magnificence et du jeu des décorations, nous n'aurions pas la force de nous refuser à la connaissance de l'ouvrier éternel qui a préparé le spectacle: mais qui s'avise de s'émerveiller de ce qu'il voit depuis cinquante ans? Les uns, occupés de leurs besoins, n'ont guère eu le temps de se livrer à des spéculations métaphysiques; le lever de l'astre du jour les appelait au travail; la plus belle nuit, la nuit la plus touchante etait muette pour eux, ou ne leur disait autre chose, sinon qu'il était l'heure du repos. Les autres, moins occupés, ou n'ont jamais eu l'occasion d'interroger la nature, ou n'ont pas eu l'esprit d'entendre sa réponse. Le génie philosophe, dont la sagacité, secouant le joug de l'habitude, s'étonna le premier des prodiges qui l'environnaient, descendit en lui-même, se demanda et se rendit raison de tout ce qu'il voyait, a pu se faire attendre longtemps, et mourir sans avoir accrédité ses opinions.

In this note, Diderot has moved from the context of Shaftesbury's point ("That it is possible for a creature capable of using reflection to have a liking or dislike of moral actions, and consequently a sense of right and wrong, before such time as he may have any settled notion of a God, is what will hardly be questioned"; *Inquiry*, 266) to a statement about "natural" atheism ("Qu'une société d'hommes n'ait eu ni dieux, ni autels, ni même de nom dans sa langue pour désigner un Etre suprême....") to an assessment of man's inability to *see* God's handiwork.

Earlier, in two successive notes (note 1, page 26, note 1, page 27), the problem of the demonstrability of order in nature poses itself.

> Dans l'univers tout est uni. Cette vérité fut un des premiers pas de la philosophie, et ce fut un pas de géant. *Ac mihi quidem veteres illi majus quiddam animo complexi, multo plus etiam vidisse videntur, quam quantum nostrorum acies intueri potest; qui omnia haec quae supra et subter, unam esse et una vi, atque una consensione naturae constricta esse dixerunt. Nullum est enim genus rerum quod aut avulsum a coeteris per seipsum constare, aut quo coetera si careant, vim suam atque aeternitatem conservare possint.* Cic. Lib. III, *de Orat*. Toutes les découvertes des philosophes modernes se réunissent pour constater la même proposition. Tous les auteurs de

> systèmes, sans en excepter Epicure, la supposaient, lorsqu'ils ont considéré le monde comme une machine, dont ils avaient à expliquer les ressorts secrets. Plus on voit loin dans la nature, et plus on y voit d'union. Il ne nous manque qu'une intelligence, et des expériences proportionnées à la multitude des parties et à la grandeur du tout, pour parvenir à la démonstration. Mais si le tout est immense, si le nombre des parties est infini, devons-nous être surpris que cette union nous échappe souvent? Quelle raison a-t-on d'en conclure qu'elle ne subsiste pas? Je ne vois pas comment ce phénomène fatal à cette espèce est, par une suite de l'ordre universel des choses, avantageux à une autre espèce, donc l'ordre universel est une chimère. Voila le raisonnement de ceux qui attaquent la nature. Voici maintenant la réponse et le raisonnement de ceux qui la défendent: je suis en état de démontrer que ce qui fait en mille occasions le mal d'un système, se tourne, par une suite merveilleuse de l'ordre universel, à l'avantage d'un autre; donc, lorsque je n'ai pas la même évidence, par rapport à d'autres phénomènes semblables, ce n'est point l'altération dans l'ordre, mais insuffisance dans mes lumières; donc l'ordre universel des choses n'en est pas moins réel et parfait. Entre la présomption raisonnable de ceux-ci et l'ignorante témérité de leurs antagonistes, il n'est pas difficile de prendre parti. (*Essai*, note 1, p. 26; italics in Diderot's text)

As Venturi has noted, "la citation de Cicéron est empruntée aux *Moralists*," and he adds that "La reste n'est qu'un remaniement des pages qui viennent immédiatement après" (Venturi, *op. cit.*, p. 346). However, a confrontation of these two texts — Diderot's note and the "source" passages of *The Moralists* — reveals a few interesting differences.

> All things in this world are united. For as the branch is united with the tree, so is the tree as immediately with the earth, air, and water which feed it.... [4] See there the

---

[4] We note that, instead of adopting Shaftesbury's biological metaphor for universal union, Diderot speaks of *mechanism*: ".... le monde comme une machine." Similarly, elsewhere on page 26, in the text of the *Essai*, "Tous les animaux composent un système, et ce système est soumis à des lois *mécaniques*, selon lesquelles tout ce qui y entre est *calculé*" (Shaftesbury: ".... there is a system of all animals: an animal-order or economy, according to which the animal affairs are regulated and disposed"; *Inquiry*, 246).

mutual dependency of things? the relation of one to another; of the sun to this inhabited earth, and of the earth and other planets to the sun? the order, union, and coherence of the whole? and know, my ingenious friend, that by this survey you will be obliged to own the universal system and coherent scheme of things to be established on *abundant proof*, capable of convincing any fair and just contemplator of the works of Nature. For scarce would any one, till he had well surveyed this universal scene, believe a union *thus evidently demonstrable*, by such numerous and powerful instances of mutual correspondency and relation, from the minutest ranks and orders of beings to the remotest spheres. (*Moralists*, 64-65)

We should now consider the passages of the *Inquiry* to which Diderot's notes on pages 26 and 27 are appended:

Now, if the whole system of animals, together with that of vegetables, and all other things in this inferior world, be properly comprehended in one system of a globe or earth, and if, again, this globe or earth itself appears to have a real dependence on something still beyond, as, for example, either on its sun, the galaxy, or its fellow-planets, then is it in reality a part only of some other system. And if it be allowed that there is in like manner a system of all things, and a universal nature, there can be no particular being or system which is not either good or ill in that general one of the universe; for if it be insignificant and of no use, it is a fault or imperfection, and consequently ill in the general system.

Therefore if any being be wholly and really ill, it must be ill with respect to the universal system; and then the system of the universe is ill or imperfect. But if the ill of one private system be the good of others; if it makes still to the good of the general system (as when one creature lives by the destruction of another; one thing is generated from the corruption of another; or one planetary system or vortex may swallow up another), then is the ill of that private system no real ill in itself, any more than the pain of breeding teeth is ill in a system or body which is so constituted that, without this occasion of pain, it would suffer worse by being defective.

So that we cannot say of any being that it is wholly and absolutely ill, unless we can positively show and ascertain that what we call ill is nowhere good besides, in any other system, or with respect to any other order or economy whatsoever. (*Inquiry*, 246)

Shaftesbury argues here then that we cannot claim that the system of nature is faulty unless we can *demonstrate* beyond doubt the existence of absolute "ill." On the other hand, Diderot reveals, by the fact that he himself twice alludes to the incompleteness of our demonstrations, that he feels some need to modify Shaftesbury's argument. Let us not overlook the fact that, in the passage from *The Moralists* which we have cited, Shaftesbury asserts that *union* itself is "evidently demonstrable," while Diderot avows in note 1, page 26, that "cette union nous échappe souvent," and therefore more cautiously claims that, although we can in many *cases* demonstrate that "ce qui fait ... le mal d'un système, se tourne ... à l'avantage d'un autre," many phenomena are not likewise explainable.

The passage in which Diderot expresses his reservations is nevertheless paralleled to a certain extent in *The Moralists* by the following:

> "Now in this mighty union, if there be such relations of parts one to another as are not easily discovered, if on this account the end and use of things does not everywhere appear, there is no wonder, since 'tis no more indeed than what must happen of necessity; nor could supreme wisdom have otherwise ordered it. For in an infinity of things thus relative, a mind which sees not infinitely can see nothing fully; and since each particular has relation to all in general, it can know no perfect or true relation of any thing in a world not perfectly and fully known." (*Moralists*, 65)

But Shaftesbury's willing resignation to the workings of "supreme wisdom" is not matched by Diderot, and more pertinently, Shaftesbury-Theocles continues by protesting that even though our knowledge of things contains *lacunae*, we should be ultimately satisfied with our vision:

> "The same may be considered in any dissected animal, plant, or flower; where he who is no anatomist, nor versed in natural history, sees that the many parts have a relation to the whole, for thus much even a slight view affords;

but he who like you, my friend, is curious in the works of Nature, and has been let into a knowledge of the animal and vegetable world, he alone can readily declare the just relation of all these parts to one another, and the several uses to which they serve." (*Moralists*, 65-66)

I do not wish to *over*-stress Diderot's discontent with the concept of universal order, and one must admit that he too ultimately affirms that, for all our ignorance, "l'ordre universel des choses n'en est pas moins réel et parfait." Sill, it is evident that the notion remains for him a "*présomption* raisonable," not an overwhelming and unquestionable certainty. In *The Moralists*, it is Philocles, the skeptic, who confronts Theocles, the defender of a divinely ordained plan, with the need for demonstration of coherent universal order:

> This is your argument... You go (If I may say so) upon fact, and would prove that things actually are in such a state and condition, which if they really were, there would indeed be no dispute left. Your union is your main support. Yet how is it you prove this? What *demonstration* have you given? What have you so much as offered at, beyond bare probability? So far are you from *demonstrating* anything, that if this uniting scheme be the chief argument for deity (as you tacitly allow) you seem rather to have *demonstrated*, "that the case itself is incapable of *demonstration*." For, "how, say you, can a narrow mind see all things?" ... And yet if in reality it sees not all, it had as good see nothing. The *demonstrable* part is still as far behind. (*Moralists*, 70-71)

For Philocles the argument for order seems at first to be only *presumption:* "The presumption, I must confess," he says to Theocles, "by this reckoning is wholly on your side. Yet, still this is only presumption" (*Moralists*, 108). But Philocles is convinced, finally, by Theocles' argument that God's benevolence ensures the existence of perfect order:

> For whatever is possible in the whole, the nature or mind of the whole will put in execution for the whole's good; and if it be possible to exclude ill, it will exclude it. Therefore, since notwithstanding the appearances, 'tis possible that ill may actually be excluded, count upon it

"that actually it is excluded." For nothing merely passive can oppose this universally active principle. (*Moralists,* 109)

Diderot, in his adaptation in note 1, page 26 of this dialogue between Philocles and Theocles, plays *both* roles and presents *both* sides of the argument, suggesting obviously that he is not as easily convinced as Philocles.

The text of note 1, page 27, when compared with *its* "source," reveals a less apparent contrast than was the case with the above passages, but one which is similar to those with which we have already dealt. The source for the note on page 27 is to be found, again, in *The Moralists*. Theocles to Philocles:

"If you would willingly enter further into this thought, and consider *how much we ought not only to be satisfied with this our view of things, but even to admire its clearness,* imagine only some person entirely a stranger to navigation, and ignorant of the nature of the sea or waters; how great his astonishment would be, when finding himself on board some vessel, anchoring at sea, remote from all land prospect, whilst it was yet a calm, he viewed the ponderous machine firm and motionless in the midst of the smooth ocean, and considered its foundations beneath, together with its cordage, masts, and sails above. How easily would he see the whole one regular structure, all things depending on one another; the uses of the rooms below, the lodgments, and conveniences of men and stores? But being ignorant of the intent or design of all above, would he pronounce the masts and cordage to be useless and cumbersome, and for this reason condemn the frame and despise the architect? O my friend! let us not thus betray our ignorance; but consider where we are, and in what a universe. Think of the many parts of the vast machine in which we have so little insight, and of which it is impossible we should know the ends and uses, when instead of seeing to the highest pendants, we see only some lower deck, and are in this dark case of flesh, confined even to the hold and meanest station of the vessel." (*Moralists,* 66)

Shaftesbury concludes that we have enough evidence of order in nature to assume that it is the product of design. Yet Diderot's tone does not seem to correspond entirely to Shaftesbury's satisfaction with the clarity of our view of things:

> Que deviennent donc les manichéens, avec la nécessité prétendue de leurs principes? Où aboutissent les reproches que les athées font à la nature? On dirait, à les entendre dogmatiser, qu'ils sont initiés dans tous ses desseins, qu'ils ont une connaissance parfaite de ses ouvrages, et qu'ils seraient en état de se mettre au gouvernail, et de manœuvrer à sa place. Et ils ne veulent pas s'apercevoir qu'ils sont, par rapport à l'univers, dans un cas plus désavantageux qu'un de ces Mexicains, qui, ne connaissant ni la navigation, ni la nature de la mer, ni les propriétés des vents et des eaux, s'éveillerait au milieu d'un vaisseau arrêté en plein Océan par un calme profond. Que penserait-il, en considérant cette pesante machine, suspendue sur un élément sans consistance? Et que penserait-on de lui, s'il venait à traiter de poids incommodes et superflus, les ancres, les voiles, les mats, les échelles, les vergues, et tout cet attirail de cordages dont il ignorerait l'utilité? En attendant qu'il fût mieux instruit (dût-il ne l'être jamais parfaitement), ne lui siérait-il pas mieux de juger, sur les proportions qu'il remarque dans le petit nombre de parties qui sont à sa portée, plus avantageusement de l'ouvrier et du tout? (*Essai*, 27, note 1)

"En attendant qu'il fût mieux instruit (dût-il ne l'être jamais parfaitement) ...."[5] serves to qualify the rest of Diderot's last sentence, which therefore reflects, not satisfied conviction, but a judgement based upon probability. Diderot seems to say, in effect, that we have not yet gleaned enough evidence (and we may never have enough evidence) from our restricted field of observation ("le petit nombre des parties...") to conclude that order is not all-pervasive and the work of an Orderer.[6] Finally, we have noted

---

[5] An echo of the passage which we have already cited, "C'est ce que nous ne connaîtrons peut-être jamais," *Essai*, p. 23.

[6] According to Jacques Roger, "Le preuve de Dieu par l'ordre du monde devient ainsi clairement ce qu'elle n'a jamais cessé d'être, une pétition de principe dont il convient de retourner les termes: le monde est en ordre parce qu'il est l'œuvre de Dieu. Car il n'est pas nécessaire de connaître tout l'univers pour trouver cet ordre en défaut, et Diderot n'a pas attendu 1749 pour savoir qu'il y a des monstres, des 'créatures originellement imparfaites, estropiées entre les mains de la nature.' Mais en 1745 il se garde bien d'en

that Diderot has not let the question of demonstration rest with Shaftesbury's oblique statement of it in the *Inquiry*. Rather, he turned to *The Moralists*, where the problem is more amply discussed, in order to bring forth passages which give a more detailed presentation of his own views.

3. Atheism and Free-Thought.

A. *Discours préliminaire* and Textual Modifications.

"Des athées qui se piquent de probité, et des gens sans probité qui vantent leur bonheur: voilà mes adversaires," proclaims Diderot in the *Discours préliminaire* (p. 12). Thus, as regards atheism, the fundamental bias seems explicit: atheists, given to "les sophismes de l'incrédulité" (p. 12), claim falsely that they are virtuous, for there can be no virtue without a sound belief in God. One must be "stupide" (Diderot's addition, p. 22; see Shaftesbury, p. 241) in order to remain inflexibly a "parfait athée," but atheists there are, men afflicted with "idées sombres et mélancoliques" (Diderot's addition, p. 59; see Shaftesbury, p. 276). Diderot underlines the misfortunes of atheism:

As to atheism, it does not seem that it can directly have any effect at all towards the setting up a false species of right or wrong. For notwithstanding a man may through custom, or by licentiousness of practice, favoured by atheism, come in time to lose much of his natural moral sense, yet it does not seem that atheism should of itself be the cause of any estimation or valuing of anything	D'abord, il ne paraît pas que l'athéisme ait aucune influence diamétralement contraire à la pureté du sentiment naturel de la droiture et de l'injustice. Un *malheureux*, que cette hypothèse aura jeté et entretenu dans *une longue habitude de crimes*, peut avoir les idées de justice et d'honnêteté fort obscurcies; mais elle ne le conduit point par elle-meme à regarder comme grande et belle une action

---

conclure contre l'ordre du monde: il en déduit seulement que les monstres moraux ne peuvent être allégués contre la bonté de l'espèce humaine. Nous sommes encore bien loin du 'Voyez-moi bien, M. Holmes' de l'aveugle Saunderson" ("Le Déisme du jeune Diderot," in *Europäische Aufklärung: Herbert Dieckmann zum 60. Geburtstag*, ed. Friedrich and Schalk, Munich, W. Fink Verlag, 1967, pp. 238-39).

as fair, noble, and deserving, vile et déshonnête. (*Essai*, 45) which was the contrary. (*Inquiry*, 261-62).

If atheism does not lead *directly* to a perversion of values and of the moral sense, it is "moins dangereux en ceci *seulement* que la superstition" (Diderot's addition, p. 45, my emphasis; see Shaftesbury, pp. 261-262).

Free-thinkers also come in for their share of Diderot's disdain. Like Asgil, Toland, and Tindal, they may be distinguished by their bad writing as much as by their lack of Christian principles.

> .... mauvais protestants et misérables écrivains. Swift, qui s'y connait sans doute, en porte ce jugement dans son chef-d'œuvre de plaisanterie: "Aurait-on jamais soupçonné, dit-il, qu'Asgil fut un beau génie et Toland un philosophe, si la religion, ce sujet inépuisable, ne les avait pourvus abondamment d'esprit et de syllogismes? Quel autre sujet, renfermé dans les bornes de la nature et de l'art, aurait été capable de procurer à Tindal le nom d'auteur profond, et de le faire lire? Si cent plumes de cette force avaient été employées pour la défense du christianisme, elles auraient été d'abord livrées à un oubli éternel." (*Essai*, pp. 16-17) [7]

Moreover, "les beaux esprits et les gens du bel air," whose pens, in their "licence" (Shaftesbury: "freedom," *Inquiry*, p. 238), have stirred up "le camp des *dévots*," shy away from serious debate — "car les raisonneurs les effraient" (Diderot's additions, p. 18; see Shaftesbury, p. 238).

---

[7] The source for this quotation of Swift is *An Argument to Prove That the Abolishing of Christianity in England May be Attended with Some Inconveniences* (*Works*, ed. Sheridan, 1801, II, 394-95): "Who would ever have suspected Asgil for a wit, or Toland for a philosopher, if the inexhaustible stock of christianity had not been at hand, to provide them with materials? what other subject through all art or nature, could have produced Tindal for a profound author, or furnished him with readers? it is the wise choice of the subject, that alone adorns and distinguishes the writer. For, had a hundred such pens as these been employed on the side of religion, they would have immediately sunk into silence and oblivion."

B. Footnote Additions.

Material to be found in Diderot's notes generally strengthens and broadens the attack upon atheism, and therein Diderot reiterates the points that, on the one hand, many atheists reveal their own bad faith, and on the other, atheism cannot, in any case, inspire virtuous behavior.

In three instances Diderot accuses atheists of insincerity and inconsistency: is it not true, he asks, that those who decry the existence of God and of objective values are guilty of denying the reality of what they themselves experience? "Ne sont-ils pas actuellement *sous le charme?* Le plaisir de paraître sincères n'agit-il pas en eux? ne sont-ils pas affectés du *decorum et dulce*" (*Essai*, note 1, p. 33)? Lucretius, "qui a employé tous les charmes de son art pour décrier ceux de la nature, s'abandonne plus que personne aux transports, aux ravissements et à l'enthouisiasme; et, à en juger par la vivacité de ses descriptions, qui que ce soit ne fut plus sensible que lui aux beautés de l'univers" (*Essai*, note 2, p. 33). Diderot acknowledges therefore that "il y a des hommes assez déréglés pour affecter l'athéisme et l'irréligion, à qui, par conséquent, il vaudrait mieux faire honte de leur vanité ridicule que de les combattre en forme" (note 1, p. 19). Those atheists who dogmatically defend their beliefs attempt to assure us "de la meilleure foi du monde, disent-ils, 'que la Divinité n'est qu'un vain fantôme; que le vice et la vertu sont des préjugés d'éducation; que l'immortalité de l'âme, que la crainte des peines et l'espérance des récompenses à venir sont chimériques'" (*Essai*, note 1, p. 33); hence atheism presents very real dangers to the solid edifice of society: "Si tous les hommes sont une fois persuadés que les lois divines et humaines sont des barrières qu'on a tort de respecter lorsqu'on peut les franchir sans danger, il n'y aura plus de dupes que les sots" (note 1, p. 33). These remarks are followed by a rendering of Shaftesbury's "reply" to Hobbes in *An Essay on The Freedom of Wit and Humour*.

"Sir! The philosophy you have condescended to reveal to us, is most extraordinary. We are beholden to you for your instruc-	"La philosophie que vous avez la bonté de me révéler est tout à fait extraordinaire. Je vous suis obligé de vos lumières:

tion. But pray, whence is this zeal in our behalf?.... Leave us to ourselves, and to that noble art by which we are happily tamed, and rendered thus mild and sheepish. 'Tis not fit we should know that by nature we are all wolves. Is it possible that one who has really discovered himself such, should take pains to communicate such a discovery?" (Characteristics, I, 63)

mais quel intérêt prenez-vous à mon instruction? ... Abandonnez-moi à mes préjugés; il n'est bon, ni pour vous ni pour moi, que je sache que la nature m'a fait *vautour,* * et que je ne peux demeurer en conscience tel que je suis." (*Essai*, note 1, p. 33; * my italics)

As Franco Venturi and Leland Thielemann have pointed out,[8] Diderot, in his translation of this passage, removes the most obvious allusions to the moral philosophy of Hobbes (e.g. "vautours" is substituted for "wolves," the tell-tale *homo homini lupus* of Hobbes). Diderot deliberately does so, I feel,[9] in order to exempt Hobbes from the general condemnation placed upon atheists in this note, for the case of Hobbes is adduced, in fact, as an *exception* to the rule in note 2, page 58.

Note 2, page 58 is appended as commentary to Shaftesbury's "Now as to atheism; though it be plainly deficient and without remedy, in the case of ill judgment on the happiness of virtue, yet it is not, indeed, of necessity the cause of any such ill judgment" (*Inquiry,* 275). Diderot begins his remarks with a categorical statement: "L'athéisme laisse la probité sans appui. Il fait pis, il pousse indirectement à la dépravation." Yet — "Cependant" — Hobbes "était bon citoyen, bon parent, bon ami, et ne croyait point en Dieu."[10] In other words, the case of Hobbes is

---

[8] Venturi, *La Jeunesse,* p. 350; Leland Thielemann, "Diderot and Hobbes," *Diderot Studies II,* ed. Fellows and Torrey, Syracuse U. Press, 1952, pp. 221-278.

[9] In this I differ with Thielemann, *loc. cit.,* p. 222, who remarks that it is "questionable" that Diderot "deliberately concealed Hobbes' identity as the author Shaftesbury was refuting."

[10] Diderot's description of Hobbes, as other critics have noted, seems to have been inherited from Bayle: "Sa longue vie a toujours été celle d'un parfaitement honnête homme. Il aimait sa patrie, il etait fidèle à son roi, bon ami, charitable, officieux. Il a néanmoins passé pour athée; mais ceux qui ont fait sa vie soutiennent qu'il avait des opinions très orthodoxes sur

counter-evidence: his example indicates that atheists have been known to be virtuous. I shall cite here one more bit of evidence from the text of Diderot's translation which might further suggest that his attitude towards the idea of "l'athée vertueux" is more equivocal than it might at first appear.

We have known people who ... have paid little regard to religion, and have been considered as mere atheists, have yet been observed to practise the rules of morality, and act in many cases with such good meaning and affection towards mankind as *might seem* to force an acknowledgement of their being virtuous. (*Inquiry*, 237)	N'a-t-on pas vu des peuples qui ... se piquaient si peu d'être religieux, qu'on les regarde comme de vrais athées, observaient les grands principes de la morale, *et nous ont arraché l'épithète de vertueux*, par la tendresse et l'affection généreuse qu'ils ont eues pour le genre humain. (*Essai*, 17)

The modification in the above passage suggests that for Diderot virtuous behavior in non-believers is not simply a hypothetical question. The fact that Diderot alludes to and concurs with Bayle's opinion of Hobbes clashes with Shaftesbury's enthusiastic condemnation of Hobbes's ideas, and would indicate that Diderot harbors some reservations, if not about the theoretical negative aspects of atheism in general, at least about the virtue of *some* atheists.

I have tried to show that Diderot's translation of the passages of the *Inquiry* which have to do with atheism, theism, and deism contains modifications which indicate that his convictions are frequently less firm in these matters than Shaftesbury's. Especially in the cases of the vision of universal order and the moral worth of atheists, Diderot's opinions differ significantly from those of his English counterpart and show that he is struggling with these problems himself, and already approaching later developments of his thought.

---

la nature de Dieu" (*Dictionnaire historique et critique*, article "Hobbes," Rotterdam, 1715, II, p. 483).

II. Religious Fanaticism.

1. "A mon frère" and Textual Modifications.

Since Diderot prefaces his translation of the Inquiry with the letter "A mon frère," where he severely criticizes religious fanaticism, we should expect that a large number of the additions and modifications in the Essai would have to do with various excesses of religious institutions and practice. In attacking, in his dedicatory letter, religious fanaticism, and opposing it to a humanistic "zèle éclairé," Diderot announces fundamental themes which will reappear in several additions and modifications in the Essai itself. In "A mon frère," Diderot defines religious "barbarie" as "cette sombre disposition qui rend un homme insensible aux charmes de la nature et de l'art, et aux douceurs de la société." He charges that men have, in the name of religion, perverted themselves and turned their backs on *natural* values: ".... nés avec cet enjoûment qui répand un coloris de finesse sur la raison, et d'aménité sur les vertus, ils l'ont émoussé, l'ont perdu, et sont parvenus, rare et sublime effort! jusqu'à fuir comme des monstres ceux qu'il leur est ordonné d'aimer" ("A mon frère," p. 9). Those who have succeeded in stifling their humanity have divided their country and perpetrated atrocities in attempting to impose their will upon others: ".... rappelez-vous l'histoire de nos troubles civils, et vous verrez la moitié de la nation se baigner dans le sang de l'autre moitié, et violer, pour soutenir la cause de Dieu, les premiers sentiments de l'humanité; comme s'il fallait cesser d'être homme pour se montrer *religieux*" ("A mon frère," p. 10)! The dangers of fanaticism having been made clear, Diderot now asserts that there is in fact no antagonism between virtue and a "zèle éclairé," that "La religion et la morale ont des liaisons trop étroites pour qu'on puisse faire contraster leurs principes fondamentaux. Point de vertu sans religion..." ("A mon frère," p. 10). But this defense of a firm link between virtuous behavior and religious faith is not always so vigorous in many cases in Diderot's additions to the text itself, to the extent that the excesses of Christian dogma and superstition are shown to be irrational, unnatural, and inhuman. To claim that religious people are not always virtuous and that virtuous men are not always practicing members of a religious sect is of course not identical with declaring that moral worth can be attained independent of a belief in God. Upon this last question, as we have seen in the preceding section, Diderot is less certain of himself than he is with regard to the relationship between *organized religion* and virtue.

The modifications present in the very first pages of the *Essai* quickly indicate that Diderot wishes to emphasize the primary importance of moral principles at the expense of the value of religious belief. Here is the first paragraph of the *Inquiry*:

> Religion and Virtue appear in many respects so nearly related, that they are generally presumed inseparable companions. And so willing we are to believe well of their union, that we hardly allow it just to speak or even think of them apart. It may however be questioned whether the practice of the world in this respect be answerable to our speculation. 'Tis certain that we sometimes meet with instances which seem to make against this general supposition. We have known people who, having the appearance of great zeal in religion, have yet wanted even the common affections of humanity, and shown themselves extremely degenerate and corrupt. Others again, who have paid little regard to religion, and been considered as mere atheists, have yet been observed to practise the rules of morality, and act in many cases with such good meaning and affection towards mankind as might seem to force an acknowledgement of their being virtuous. And in general, we find mere moral principles of such weight, that in our dealings with men we are seldom satisfied by the fullest assurance given us of their zeal in religion, till we hear something further of their character. If we are told a man is religious, we still ask, "What are his morals?" But if we hear at first that he has honest moral principles, and is a man of natural justice and good temper, we seldom think of the other question, "Whether he be religious and devout?" (*Inquiry*, 237-38)

But Diderot's rendering of the first paragraph of the *Inquiry* causes the relationship between religion and virtue to seem more tenuous than it appears in Shaftesbury's text. Diderot quickly points out that cases of misconduct in believers is not lacking: where Shaftesbury says only that "we *sometimes* meet with instances which seem to make against this general supposition," Diderot shows less reserve—"La religion et la vertu sont unies par tant de rapports, qu'on les regarde communément comme deux inséparables compagnes.... Je doute cependant que cette idée scrupuleuse soit confirmée par la connaissance du monde; et *nous ne manquons pas d'exemples* qui paraissent contredire cette union prétendue" (*Essai*, 17). Accordingly, Shaftesbury notes that some pious *individuals* ("We have known some people....") are seen to be nonetheless "extremely degenerate and corrupt," but Diderot magnifies the prevalence of this phenomenon by charging that it involves *groups* of people: "N'a-t-on pas vu des *peuples* qui, avec tout le zèle imaginable pour leur religion, vivaient dans la dernière dépravation et n'avaient pas ombre d'humanité...." Shaftesbury somewhat carefully says that "we are *seldom* satisfied by the fullest assurance given us of their zeal in religion....," but Diderot proclaims that "En général, on a beau nous assurer qu'un homme est plein de zèle pour sa religion, si nous avons à traiter avec lui, nous nous informons encore de son caractère." And again, shortly thereafter: "But if we hear at first that he has honest moral principles, and is a man of natural justice and good temper, we *seldom* think of the other question..." becomes "Si vous m'eussiez fait entendre d'abord qu'il était honnête homme, je ne me serais *jamais* avisé de demander s'il était dévot." It is to be noted that "TANT EST GRANDE SUR NOS ESPRITS L'AUTORITÉ DES PRINCIPES MORAUX" is placed strategically at the *end* of Diderot's paragraph as a conclusion, while in Shaftesbury's text the passage "we find mere moral principles of such weight" only introduces the last paragraph.

Shaftesbury uses the words "religious" and "devout" without any apparent distinction, but Diderot's "dévot" is not a precise equivalent of "devout," since Diderot means the word to have a pejorative connotation, to which he calls the reader's attention in note 2, page 18. In the following paragraph on page 18, where it is a question of past polemics between those who defend religion and those who attack it, Diderot replaces the affectively neutral "the religious part of mankind" with the derogatory "le camp des *dévots*" ("dévots" is again italicized by Diderot), and he describes this group more incisively than Shaftesbury:

For so much is the religious part of mankind alarmed by the *freedom* of some late pens, and *so great a jealousy* is raised everywhere on this account.... (*Inquiry*, 238)	La *licence* * de quelques plumes modernes a répandu l'alarme dans le camp des *dévots:* telle est en eux *l'aigreur et l'animosité* * .... (*Essai*, 18; * denotes my italics)

In one noteworthy case, where Shaftesbury uses "devout," Diderot substitutes "religieux."

For 'tis evident in the case of the most *devout* people, even by their own confession, that there are times when their faith can hardly support them in the belief of a supreme Wisdom, and that they are often tempted to judge disadvantageously of a providence and just administration in the whole. (*Inquiry*, 241)	De l'aveu même des personnes les plus *religieuses,* toute leur foi leur suffit à peine, en certains moments, pour les soutenir dans la conviction d'une intelligence suprême; il est des conjonctures où, frappées des défauts apparents de l'administration de l'univers, elles sont violemment tentées de juger désavantageusement de la Providence. (*Essai*, 21-22)

I have presented these passages again in order to make the context fully clear. Diderot does not translate "devout" as "dévot" because he is aware that "dévot" denotes insincere religious devotion; it would mean little in this context to say that the *poseurs* in religion sometimes waver in their beliefs, since this is to be expected. He therefore translates "the most devout people" as ".... personnes les plus religieuses" in order to convey the idea that even the most sincerely faithful experience some crises of doubt about the nature of things.

Shaftesbury himself speaks of "superstition," but in some instances Diderot substitutes "superstition" for "belief" or "religion."

.... even by means of the most extravagant belief or opinion in the world. (*Inquiry*, 261)	La plus extravagante *superstition*.... (*Essai*, 44)
For wherever anything, in its nature odious and abominable, is by religion advanced.... (*Inquiry*, 262)	.... car toutes les fois que ... la *superstition* exige quelque action détestable.... (*Essai*, 46)

If there be a religion.... (*Inquiry*, 263)	Si la *superstition*.... (*Essai*, 46)

In several cases, Diderot brings the argument to bear specifically upon religion, where Shaftesbury is not so precise.

'Tis otherwise in what relates to opinion, belief, or speculation.... and every action grounded on this belief, would be iniquitous, wicked, and vicious action. (*Inquiry*, 253)	Il n'en est pas ainsi (des opinions qu'on adopte, des idées qu'on se fait, ou des *religions* qu'on professe.... et toute action fondée sur des dogmes *pareils* ne peut être qu'injuste, abominable, et maudite. (*Essai*, 36-37)

The changes that Diderot makes here render explicit the analogy between the superstitions already described and *other* religions — Christianity, for example. Similarly:

Sense of right and wrong therefore being as natural to us as natural affection itself, and being a first principle in our constitution and make, there is no speculative opinion, persuasion, or belief, which is capable immediately or directly to exclude or destroy it. (*Inquiry*, 260)	Le sentiment d'injustice et d'équité nous étant aussi naturel que nos affections, cette qualité étant un des premiers éléments de notre constitution, il n'y a point de spéculation, de croyance, de persuasion, de *culte* capable de l'anéantir immédiatement et directement. (*Essai*, 43)

Diderot later elaborates Shaftesbury's opinion of formal speculation on the existence of God:

.... it being a thing not expected, or any way possible, that a creature such as man, arising from his childhood slowly and gradually to several degrees of reason and reflection, should at the very first be taken up with those speculations or more refined sort of reflections, about the subject of God's existence. (*Inquiry*, 266)	En effet, conçoit-on qu'un être tel que l'homme, en qui la faculté de penser et de réfléchir s'étend par des degrés insensibles et lents, soit, moralement parlant, assez exercé, au sortir du berceau, pour sentir la justesse et la liaison de ces spéculations *déliées*, et de ces raisonnements subtils et *métaphysiques* sur l'existence d'un Dieu? (*Essai*, 50)

Accordingly, near the end of Part I of the *Inquiry*, where Shaftesbury describes the nature of "perfect daemonism" and the conception of God as a willful tyrant, Diderot concentrates upon the attributes of such an unjust, capricious being, and thus associates a Jansenist God with more primitive deities.

We know very well that, in some religions, there are those who expressly give no other idea of God than of a being arbitrary, violent, causing ill and ordaining to misery; which in effect is the same as to substitute a daemon or devil in his room. (*Inquiry*, 242)	Nous n'ignorons pas que, dans quelques religions, on ne regarde Dieu que comme un être violent, *despotique*, arbitraire et destinant les créatures à un malheur *inévitable, sans aucun mérite ou démérite prévu:* c'est-à-dire qu'on élève un diable sur ces autels où l'on croit adorer un Dieu. (*Essai*, 22-23; the italics are mine and they represent the expressions which have no equivalent in Shaftesbury's passage)

In the first section of Part II, Diderot's modifications emphasize the dangers of inept religious counsel:

> If it be said, perhaps, that in the case before us, religious affection or devotion is a sufficient and proper remedy, we answer, that 'tis according as the kind may happily prove. For if it be of the pleasant and cheerful sort, 'tis of the very kind of natural affection itself; if it be of the dismal or fearful sort; if it brings along with it any affection opposite to manhood, generosity, courage, or free thought, there will be nothing gained by this application, and the remedy will, in the issue, be undoubtedly found worse than the disease. The severest reflections on our duty, and the consideration merely of what is by authority and under penalties enjoined, will not by any means serve to calm us on this occasion. The more dismal our thoughts are on such a subject, the worse our temper will be, and the readier to discover itself in harshness and austerity. If perhaps by compulsion, or through any necessity or fear incumbent, a different carriage be at any time affected, or different maxims owned, the practice at the bottom will be still the same. If the countenance be composed, the heart, however, will not be changed. The ill passion may for the time be withheld

from breaking into action, but will not be subdued, or in the least debilitated against the next occasion. So that in such a breast as this, whatever devotion there may be, 'tis likely there will in time be little of an easy spirit or good temper remaining, and consequently few and slender enjoyments of a mental kind. (*Inquiry*, 303)

Diderot first expands "For if it be of the pleasant and cheerful sort, 'tis of the very kind of natural affection itself":

> Dans ces dispositions fâcheuses, dira-t-on peut-être, la religion est d'un puissant secours. Sans doute; mais quelle espèce de religion? Si sa nature est consolante et bénigne; si la dévotion qu'elle inspire est douce, tranquille et gaie; c'est une affection naturelle qui ne peut être que salutaire.... (*Essai*, 87)

He thus renders more salient the contrast between a "dévotion enjouée" and somber, dangerous religious spirit. Following this, Diderot's modifications direct the blame for the corruption of beneficial religious feeling upon "les ministres":

> .... mais les ministres, en l'altérant, la rendent-ils sombre et farouche; les craintes et l'effroi l'accompagnent-ils; combat-elle la fermeté, le courage et la liberté de l'esprit; c'est entre leurs mains un dangereux topique; et l'on remarque à la longue que ce précieux remède, mal à propos administré, est pire que le mal.

This point is reinforced immediately by the bitter references to the methods of the ministers:

> La considération effrayante de l'étendue de nos devoirs, un examen austère des mortifications qui nous sont prescrites, et la vue des gouffres ouverts pour les infracteurs de la loi ne sont pas toujours et en tout temps, ni pour toutes de personnes indictinctement, des objets propres à calmer les agitations de l'esprit.[11]

---

[11] Perhaps an echo of *De rerum natura* I, 102-109:

> Tutemet a nobis quouis tempore uatum
> terriloquis uictus dictis desciscere quares.
> Quippe etenim quam multa tibi iam fingere possunt

The presentation of such visions has no positive effect on the man of a vicious character; his problems are only intensified and his character remains unchanged:

> ....Le tigre est enchaîné pour un moment; ses actions[ne] [12] décèlent pas actuellement sa férocité: mais en est-il plus soumis? Si vous brisez sa chaîne, en sera-t-il moins cruel? Non certes. Qu'a donc opéré la religion si maladroitement présentée? La créature a le même fonds de tristesse; ses aigreurs n'en sont que plus abondantes et plus importunes, et ses plaisirs intellectuels que plus languissants et plus rares. *Le chien est donc revenu à son vomissement,* mais plus maladif et plus dépravé.

In another instance, similar in context and import to the above, Diderot again stresses the excesses of devotion and inserts himself a long passage describing the just sort of religious feeling.

> This may well be allowed true in all other respects, since even religion itself, considered as a passion, not of the selfish but nobler kind, may in some characters be strained beyond its natural proportion, and be said also to be in too high a degree. For as the end of religion is to render us more perfect and accomplished in all moral duties and performances; if by the height of devout ecstasy and contemplation we are rather disabled in this respect, and rendered more unapt to the real duties and offices of civil life, it may be said that religion indeed is then too strong in us. For how, possibly, can we call this superstition, whilst the object of the devotion is acknowledged just and the faith orthodox? 'Tis only the excess of zeal which in this case is so transporting as to render the devout person more remiss in secular affairs, and less concerned for the inferior and temporal interests of mankind. (*Inquiry,* 287)

Diderot, in his version, first omits "For the end of religion is to render us more perfect and accomplished in all moral duties and

---

        somnia quae uitae rationes uertere possint,
        fortunasque tuas omnis turbare timore!
        Et merito. Nam si certam finem esse uiderent
        aerumnarum homines, aliqua ratione ualerent
        religionibus atque minis obsistere uatum.

[12] Assézat-Tourneux has "de."

performances," thus leaving aside praise of the merits of religion. This he does in order to lend more weight to the "contemplation immodérée des choses célestes" in the phrase which follows. The notion of corruption is presented in the addition ".... un zèle saint *dans son origine.*"

> On peut avouer sans crainte ces principes dans toute leur étendue, puisque la religion même, considérée comme une passion, mais de l'espèce héroïque, peut être poussée trop loin et troubler, par son excès, toute l'économie des inclinations sociales. Oui, la religion, j'ose le dire, serait trop énergique en celui qu'une *contemplation immodérée des choses célestes, qu'une intempérance d'extase* refroidirait sur les offices de la vie civile et les devoirs de la société. Cependant, "Si l'objet de la dévotion est raisonnable, et si la croyance est orthodoxe, quelle que soit la dévotion, pourra-t-on dire encore: Il est dur de la traiter de la superstition? car enfin, si la créature laisse aller ses affaires domestiques à l'abandon, et néglige les intérêts temporels de son prochain et les siens, c'est l'excès d'un zèle *saint dans son origine,* qui produit ces effets. (*Essai*, 71)

The last lines of the passage, as we have said, have no equivalent in Shaftesbury, and here Diderot makes explicit the opposition which he has previously suggested: he pronounces as "la vraie religion" a humanistic faith which prescribes a *balanced* respect for the temporal and supernatural:

> Je réponds à cela que la vraie religion ne commande pas une abnégation totale des soins ici-bas: ce qu'elle exige, c'est la préférence du cœur; elle veut qu'on rende à Dieu, aux autres et à soi-même tout ce qu'on leur doit, sans remplir une de ces obligations, au préjudice d'une autre. Elle sait les concilier entre elles par une subordination mesurée.

Scorn for immoderate interest in supra-terrestial goods is evident in the following modifications.

> On this account, all other affections towards friends, relations, or mankind are often slightly regarded, as being worldly and of little moment in respect of the interest of our soul. And so little thought is there of any immediate

> satisfaction arising from such good offices of life, that it is customary with many devout people zealously to decry all temporal advantages of goodness, all natural benefits of virtue, and magnifying the contrary happiness of a vicious state, to declare "that except only for the sake of future reward and fear of punishment, they would divest themselves of all goodness at once, and freely allow themselves to be most immoral and profligate." From whence it appears that in some respects there can be nothing more fatal to virtue than the weak and uncertain belief of a future reward and punishment. (*Inquiry*, 274-75)

The evil effects of an excessive longing for eternal rewards are magnified by Diderot:

> Une créature possédée d'un intérêt si particulier et si grand, pourrait compter le reste pour rien; et, tout occupé de son salut éternel, traiter quelquefois comme des distractions *méprisables* et des *affections viles*, terrestres et momentanées, les douceurs de l'amitié, les lois du sang et les devoirs de l'humanité. Une imagination frappée de la sorte décriera peut-être les avantages temporels de la bonté, et les récompenses naturelles de la vertu; élevera jusqu'aux nues la félicité des méchants, et déclarera, *dans les accès d'un zèle inconsidéré*, que, "sans l'attente des biens futurs et sans la crainte des peines éternelles, elle reconcerait à la probité pour se livrer entièrement à la débauche, au crime et à la dépravation." Ce qui démontre que *rien*, en quelque façon, ne serait plus fatal à la vertu qu'une croyance incertaine et vague des récompenses et des châtiments à venir. (*Essai*, 58)

And, in the last sentence of the paragraph, his condemnation of such an attitude is more firm (*"rien ... ne serait plus fatal à la vertu"*).

Perverted devotion leads to violence, as Diderot reminded his brother, and in additions to Shaftesbury's text, Diderot describes the bloodshed caused by religion in the same terms he used in "A mon frère."

.... Man, notwithstanding the assistance of religion and the direction of laws, is often found to live in less conformity with	Avec le secours de la religion et sous l'autorité des lois, l'homme vit d'une façon moins conforme à sa nature que ne font

Nature, and by means of religion itself is often rendered the more barbarous and inhuman. Marks are set on men; distinctions formed; opinions decreed under the severest penalties; antipathies instilled, and aversions raised in men against the generality of their own species. So that 'tis hard to find in any region a human society which has human laws. No wonder if in such societies 'tis so hard to find a man who lives naturally and as a man. (*Inquiry*, 292)

ces insectes. Ces lois, dont le but est de l'affermir dans la pratique de la justice, *sont souvent pour lui des sujets de révolte;* et cette religion, qui tend à le sanctifier, le rend quelquefois la plus barbare des créatures. *On propose des questions, on se chicane sur des mots*, on forme des distinctions, on passe aux dénominations odieuses, on proscrit de pures opinions sous des peines sévères: de là naissent les antipathies, les haines et les *séditions*. *On en vient aux mains; et l'on voit à la fin la moitié de l'espèce se baigner dans le sang de l'autre moitié.* J'oserais assurer qu'il est presque impossible de trouver sur la terre une société d'hommes qui se gouvernent par des principes humains. (*Essai*, 76)

The changes made in the above cited paragraph are, I think, of unusual importance, for they indicate Diderot's intense hostility towards religious institutions (the allusion to "ces lois, dont le but est d'affermir...." will be given greater attention in the following section). Diderot initially replaces "notwithstanding" with "*Avec le secours de la religion*...," thus changing the sense of the sentence in order to imply that religion and laws have *contributed* to man's corruption. There is further allusion to the vanity of theological hair-splitting ("on propose des questions, on se chicane sur des mots...."), and, as we have noted, to religious wars. Most interesting, however, are the two references to *revolt* against political and religious authority: "Ces lois ... sont souvent pour lui des sujets de *révolte*," and ".... de là naissent les antipathies, les haines et les *séditions*." A second like example is found on pages 38-39 of the *Essai*:

And thus we find how far worth and virtue depend upon a knowledge of right and wrong,

Concluons donc que le mérite ou la vertu dépendent d'une connaissance de la justice et

and on a use of reason, sufficient to secure a right application of the affections; that nothing horrid or unnatural, nothing unexemplary, nothing destructive of that natural affection by which the species or society is upheld, may on any account, or through any principle or notion of honour or religion, be at any time affected or prosecuted as a good and proper object of esteem. For such a principle as this must be wholly vicious; and whatsoever is acted upon it can be no other than vice and immorality. And thus if there be anything which teaches men either treachery, ingratitude, or cruelty, by divine warrant or under colour and pretense of any present or future good to mankind; if there be anything which teaches men to persecute their friends through love, or to torment captives of war in sport, or to offer human sacrifice, or to torment, macerate, or mangle themselves in a religious zeal before their God, or to commit any sort of barbarity or brutality as amiable or becoming; be it custom which gives applause; or religion which gives a sanction; this is not, nor ever can be, virtue of any kind, or in any sense, but must remain still horrid depravity, notwithstanding any fashion, law, custom or religion which may be ill or vicious itself, but can never alter the eternal measures and immutable independent nature of worth and virtue. (*Inquiry*, 255)

d'une fermeté de raison, capables de nous diriger dans l'emploi de nos affections. Notions de la justice, courage de la raison, ressources uniques dans le danger où l'on se trouve de consacrer ses efforts, et de prostituer son estime à des abominations, à des horreurs, à des idées destructives de toute affection naturelle. Affections naturelles, fondements de la société, que les *lois sanguinaires d'un point d'honneur* et *les principes erronés d'une fausse religion,* tendent quelquefois à saper. Lois et principes qui sont vicieux, et ne conduiront ceux qui les suivent qu'au crime et à la dépravation, puisque la justice et la raison les combattent. Quoi que ce soit donc qui, sous prétexte d'un bien présent ou futur, prescrive aux hommes, de la part de Dieu, la trahison, l'ingratitude et les cruautés; quoi que ce soit qui leur apprenne à persécuter leurs semblables par bonne amitié, à tourmenter par passetemps leurs prisonniers de guerre, à *souiller les autels de sang humain,* à se tourmenter eux-mêmes, à se macérer cruellement, à se déchirer en presence de leurs divinités; et à commettre, pour les honorer ou pour leur complaire, quelque action inhumaine et brutale; *qu'ils refusent d'obéir,* s'ils sont vertueux, et *qu'ils ne permettent point* aux *vains* applaudissements de la coutume, ou aux *oracles imposteurs de la superstition,* d'étouffer les cris de la nature et les conseils de la vertu. Toutes ces actions, que

> l'humanité proscrit, seront toujours des horreurs, en dépit des coutumes *barbares*, des lois *capricieuses*, et des *faux* cultes qui les auront ordonnés. Mais rien ne peut altérer les lois éternelles de la justice. (*Essai*, 38-39)

And again on page 46, where Diderot draws our attention to the tyranny of "superstition," and presents vividly the believer who comes to see that his God is unjust:

> Nor is this a wonder. For wherever anything, in its nature odious and abominable, is by religion advanced, as the supposed will or pleasure of a supreme Deity, if in the eye of the believer it appears not indeed in any respect the less ill and odious on this account, then must the Deity of necessity bear the blame, and be considered as a being naturally ill and odious, however courted and sollicited through mistrust and fear. But this is what religion, in the main, forbids us to imagine. It everywhere prescribes esteem and honour in company with worship and adoration. Whensoever therefore it teaches the love and admiration of a Deity who has any apparent character of ill, it teaches at the same time a love and admiration of that ill, and causes that to be taken for good and amiable which is in itself horrid and detestable. (*Inquiry*, 262)

> Et je ne vois point en cela de prodige; car toutes les fois que, sous l'autorité prétendue ou le bon plaisir des dieux, la *superstition* exige quelque action détestable; *si, malgré le voile sacré dont on l'enveloppe, le fidèle en pénètre l'énormité, de quel œil verra-t-il les objets de son culte?* En portant au pied de leurs autels des offrandes que la crainte lui arrache, il les traitera dans le fond de son cœur comme des tyrans odieux et méchants; mais c'est ce que sa religion lui défend expressément de penser. "Les dieux ne se contentent pas d'encens, lui crie-t-elle; il faut que l'estime accompagne l'hommage." Le voilà *forcé* d'aimer et d'admirer des êtres qui lui paraissent injustes; de respecter leurs commandements, *d'accomplir en aveugle* les crimes qu'ils ordonnent, et par conséquent de prendre pour saint et pour bon ce qui est en soi horrible et détestable." (*Essai*, 46)

The above examples are not, as we shall see, the only instances of Diderot's insinuating allusions to the overthrow of unjust institutions into Shaftesbury's text.

2. Footnote Additions.

The notes to the text of the *Essai* contain material which repeats the themes of the modifications listed above: the excesses of superstition and of asceticism, the violence caused by religious differences, and the notion of rebellion against tyrannical authority.

Note 1, page 37, a citation from Juvenal — "O sanctus [sic] gentes, quibus haec nascuntur in hortis/Numina" [13] — simply reinforces the point made in the text against the extremes of religious superstition. And appended to the text: "Si Jupiter est le Dieu qu'on adore, et si son histoire le représente d'un tempérament amoureux, et se livrant sans pudeur à toute l'étendue de ses désirs, il est constant qu'en prenant ce recit à la lettre, son adorateur doit regarder l'impudicité comme une vertu" (*Essai*, 46) is a citation from *Eunuchus*, III, v, where Charea indeed describes the lubricity of Jupiter. Diderot comments: "Exprimer les sentiments et les mœurs d'un peuple dans sa conduite ordinaire et familière, c'est le propre de la comédie, et dans Térence surtout. Or, voici ce que le poète fait dire à un jeune libertin, qui se sert de l'exemple de ses dieux, pour justifier une vile métamorphose, et s'encourager à une action infame" (*Essai*, 46, not 2). The passage from Petronius (the fragment "Eumolpus"), cited in the same note, deals with the people who attempt to bribe even the gods: "Ne bonam quidam mentem aut bonam valetudinem petunt: sed statim, antequam limen Capitoli tangunt, alius donum promittit, si propinquam divitem extulerit; alius, si ad trecenties H. S. salvus pervenerit. Ipse senatus, reci bonique praeceptor, mille pondo auri Capitolio promittere solet; et ne quis dubitet pecuniam concupiscere, Jovem quoque peculio exorat."

The verse from *Iphigénie* cited in note 1, page 46 is a speech of Agamemnon to Iphigenie (IV, iv), destined to be sacrificed to the gods — and to the ambition and opportunism of her father.

---

[13] Cited by Shaftesbury himself, *Miscellaneous Reflections*, ed. Robertson, II, 187.

Willingness to accede to the wishes of the deity often conceals less attractive motives.[14]

Similarly, note 1, page 45, which is adapted faithfully from Locke (*Essay Concerning Human Understanding*, Bk. I, ch. ii, sec. 9), deals with the barbaric practices condoned by religions other than Christianity.

> Sans entrer dans un long détail sur cette matière, je citerai seulement deux exemples, qu'on lit chap. ii, sect. ix, page 29, de l'*Essai philosophique sur l'Entendement humain*. Il est difficile de se refuser au témoignage d'un voyageur, lorsqu'il est scellé de l'autorité d'un écrivain tel que Locke. Les Topinambous ne connaissent pas de meilleurs moyens pour aller en paradis, que de se venger cruellement de leurs ennemis, et d'en manger le plus qu'ils peuvent. Ceux que les Turcs canonisent et mettent au nombre des saints, mènent une vie qu'on ne peut rapporter sans blesser la pudeur...." *etc.* (*Essai*, 45, note 1)

Note 2, page 37 describes the nature of "les erreurs populaires" — "On aime à persuader aux autres ce que l'on croit, et l'on résiste difficilement à ce dont on voit les autres persuadés. Il est presque impossible de rejeter les opinions qui nous viennent de loin, et comme de main en main. Le moyen de donner un démenti à tant d'honnêtes gens qui nous ont précédés!" Following this is a citation from Montaigne's "Les Boîteux": "Ceux qui se sont abbruvez successivement de ces estrangetez... ont senti par les oppositions qu'on leur a faictes, où logeoit la difficulté de la persuasion, et ils ont calfeutré ces endroicts de pieces nouvelles; ils n'ont pas craind d'aiouter de leur invention, autant qu'ils le croyoient

---

[14] Diderot's allusion is to Racine's Iphigénie, but a distinct parallel is to be found in *De rerum natura* I, 80-102:

> Illud in his rebus uereor, ne forte rearis
> inpia the rationis inire elementa uiamque
> indugredi sceleris. Quod contra saepius illa
> religio peperit scelerosa atque impia facta.
> Aulide quo pacto Triuiai uirginis aram
> Iphianassai turparunt sanguine foede
> ductores Danaum delecti, prima uirorum.
> ....
> Tantum religio potuit suadere malorum!

necessaire, pour suppléer à la résistance et au défault qu'ils pensoient être en la conception d'autruy." But Diderot does *not* quote the lines which directly precede these in Montaigne's essay:

> J'ay veu la naissance de plusieurs miracles de mon temps. Encore qu'ils s'estoufent en naissant nous ne laissons pas de prévoir le train qu'ils eussent pris s'ils eussent vescu leur aage. Car il n'est que de trouver le bout du fil, on en desvite tant qu'on veut. Et y a plus loing de rien à la plus petite chose du monde, qu'il y a de celle-là jusques à la plus grande. (*Essais*, III, xi)

Diderot omits these lines because they contain explicit mention of "miracles," a word which would perhaps place the discussion of "les erreurs populaires" in a properly religious context. Still, as Diderot surely expected, the full import of Montagne's remarks would not be ignored by the attentive literate reader of the *Essai sur le mérite et la vertu*.

The distinction that Diderot makes between the expressions "religieux" and "dévot" is given greater clarity in note 2, page 18: "Partout où ce mot se prend en mauvaise part, il faut entendre, comme dans La Bruyère et La Rochefoucauld, faux dévot; sens auquel une longue et peut-être odieuse prescription l'a déterminé." Diderot's use of a footnote in order to specify the meaning of "dévot" resembles, in fact, La Bruyere's addition of notes ("faux dévot," "fausse dévotion") to the several passages in "De la mode" in which he describes "les dévots" and "la dévotion."

Note 1, page 18 expands the examination of the relationship between religion and morality.

> Remarquez qu'il est question ici de la religion en général. Si le christianisme était un culte universellement embrassé, quand on assurerait d'un homme qu'il est bon chrétien, peut-être serait-il absurde de demander s'il est honnête homme; parce qu'il n'y a point, dirait-on, de christianisme réel sans probité.

The note begins with "Remarquez...," a qualification which would seem to reassure Diderot's Christian readers. Diderot follows this with the apparently innocuous observation that it is probably true that all true Christians are "honnêtes hommes," but at the same time he has pointed out the limited influence of the Christian religion. Furthermore,

> Il y a presque autant de cultes différents que de gouvernements; et si nous en croyons les histoires, leurs préceptes croisent souvent les principes de la morale; ce qui suffit pour justifier ma pensée.

The point thus brought forth is the *multiplicity* of religious dogma as contrasted with the fundamental *universality* of "principes de la morale": religious dogma *often* clashes with the latter.

> Mais, afin de lui donner toute l'évidence possible, supposez que, dans un besoin pressant de secours, on vous adressât à quelque juif opulent: vous savez que sa religion permet l'usure avec l'étranger; espériez-vous donc traiter à des conditions plus favorables, parce qu'on vous assurerait que cet homme est un des sectateurs les plus zélés de la foi de Moïse? et tout bien considéré, ne vaudrait-il pas beaucoup mieux, pour vos intérêts, qu'il passât pour un fort mauvais juif, et qu'il fut même soupçonné dans la synagogue d'être un peu chrétien?

The example of the money-lending Jew firmly plants in the reader's mind the notion of the relativism of religious beliefs (that which is right for a Jew may be wrong for a Christian) and demonstrates that unsavory practices are condoned by religion. Finally, one is led to agree that even the most zealous believers may be unscrupulous when we measure their actions according to standards of "principes moraux" — the point that Diderot's modifications of the *text* of pages 17-18 already suggested.

On page 272 of the *Inquiry* Shaftesbury asserts that "Though a right distribution of justice in a government be so essential a cause of virtue, we must observe in this case that it is example which chiefly influences mankind, and forms the character and disposition of a people." However, in his note on page 55 of the *Essai* Diderot points out that not all *moralistes* agree with Shaftesbury on this question:

> Tous les moralistes ne sont pas de cet avis: 'Telle est, dit un d'entre eux dans son *Projet pour l'avancement de la religion*, la perversité des hommes, que le seul exemple

> d'un prince vicieux entraînera bientôt la masse générale de ses sujets, et que la conduite exemplaire d'un monarque vertueux n'est pas capable de les réformer, si elle n'est soutenue d'autres expédients. Il faut donc que le souverain, en exerçant avec vigueur l'autorité que les lois et son sceptre lui donnent, fasse en sorte qu'il soit de l'intérêt de chacun de s'attacher à la vertu, en privant les vicieux de toute espérance d'avancement.' Il est clair que ce savant auteur donne la préférence aux avantages d'une bonne administration sur ceux d'un bon exemple.

Swift's text reads as follows: "Thus human nature seems to lie under the disadvantage, that the example alone of a vicious prince, will in time corrupt an age; but the example of a good one, will not be sufficient to reform it without farther endeavors. Princes must therefore supply this defect by a vigourous exercise of that authority, which the law has left them; by making it every man's interest and honour, to cultivate *religion* and virtue; by rendering vice a disgrace, and the certain ruin to preferment or pretensions." [15] Diderot deliberately misquotes Swift in order to present virtue — not religion and virtue — as the fundamental component of a sound state.

Note 1, page 38 and note 1 page 39 both serve to define an antagonism between religious dogma and "la nature." The first of these is appended to the passage on page 38 which we have already cited above where the subject of ascetic self-mortification is broached, and Diderot argues in the note that self-torment is in no way a means to achieve virtue: this *reason* tell us:

> Domptez vos passions, dit la religion; conservez-vous, dit la nature. Il est toujours possible de satisfaire à l'une et à l'autre; du moins il faut le supposer; car il serait bien singulier qu'il y eut un cas où l'on serait forcé de devenir homicide de soi-même, pour être vertueux. C'est ce que les piétistes outrés ne manqueraient pas d'apercevoir, s'ils osaient consulter la raison.... (*Essai,* note 1, 38)

---

[15] *A Project for the Advancement of Religion and the Reformation of Manners.* In *Works,* ed. Thomas Sheridan, London, 1801. II, 405-406. My italics.

Thus the opposition is distinguished: religion exhorts us to tame our passions and to be virtuous, but nature has endowed us with an instinct for self-preservation, and reason recoils from the notion that virtue involves doing oneself bodily harm. The "piétistes outrés" would surely condemn the man who shoots himself in despair over his inability to reconcile nature and religious principles. They would also have to, logically, condemn the man who chooses to end his life less abruptly, he too being unable to resolve the conflict between his natural being and his religious beliefs, yet knowing that suicide is a mortal sin:

> Celui qui, fatigué de lutter contre lui-même, finirait la querelle d'un coup de pistolet, serait un enragé, leur dirait-elle. Mais celui qui, révolté de ce procédé brusque, prendrait, par amour de Dieu, et pour le bien de son âme, chaque jour une dose légère d'un poison qui le conduirait insensiblement au tombeau, serait-il moins fou? Non, sans doute....

But, says Diderot, the means matters not, the crime ("crime" — not "péché") remains the same:

> Si le crime est dans le suicide, qu'importe qu'on se tue par des jeûnes et des veilles, de l'arsénic ou du sublimé? dans un instant ou dans l'espace de dix années? avec un cilice et des fouets, un pistolet ou un poignard? C'est disputer sur la forme du crime; c'est s'excuser sur la couleur du poison....

Whether one uses the gestures and the tools of the ascetics or more conventional methods, suicide is suicide; to think otherwise is to employ a double standard. Diderot now adroitly turns to one of the Fathers for support in his argument, and he cites a phrase from *La Cité de Dieu* (VI, x: "De libertate Senacae, qui vehementius civilem theologian reprehendit quam Varro fabulosam"): "Telle était la pensée de saint Augustin. Ceux qui croient honorer Dieu par ces excès sont dans la même superstition que ces païens, dont il dit dans son Traité merveilleux de la *Cité de Dieu: Tantus*

54 THE SIGNIFICANCE OF DIDEROT'S "ESSAI SUR LE MÉRITE...

est pertubatae mentis et sedibus suis pulsae furor, ut sic dii placentur quaemadmodum ne homines quidem saeviunt." [16]

The "death-wish" of the fervent believer is the subject of note 1, page 102. Shaftesbury's *text* reads as follows:

> There is nothing more certain or more universally agreed than this, "that life may sometimes be even a misfortune and misery." To enforce the continuance of it in creatures reduced to much extremity is esteemed the greatest cruelty. And though religion forbids that any one should be his reliever, yet if by some fortunate accident, death offers of itself, it is embraced as highly welcome. (*Inquiry*, 317-18)

Diderot's translation:

> Que la vie soit quelquefois un malheur, c'est un fait généralement avoué. Quand une créature en est réduite à désirer la mort, c'est la traiter avec rigueur que de lui commander de vivre. Dans ces conjonctures, quoique la religion *et la raison* retiennent le bras et ne permettent pas de finir ses maux en terminant ses jours, s'il se présente quelque honnête et plausible occasion de périr, on peut l'embrasser sans scrupule. (*Essai*, 102)

Diderot shows that religion is not the only force which presents itself as an obstacle to self-annihilation. But the note, appended to ".... lui commander de vivre," serves to greatly contradict the point made in the text:

> Sans compter toutes ces catastrophes désespérantes qui rendent la vie insupportable, l'amour de Dieu produit le même effet: *Cupio dissolvi, et esse cum Christo*, disait saint Paul. Mais si Judas l'apôtre, après avoir trahi son

---

[16] Latin citation is italicized in Assézat-Tourneux. The quotation is taken from a passage in which Augustine himself quotes from Seneca's *De Superstitione:*

> De ipsis vero ritibus crudeliter turpibus quam libere scripsit! "Ille, inquit, viriles sibi partes amputat, ille lacertos secat. Ubi iratos deos timent, qui sic propitios merentur? Dii autem nullo debent coli genere, si hoc volunt." Tantus est pertubatae mentis et sedibus suis pulsae furor, ut sic dii placentur, quem ad modum ne quidem homines saeviunt taeterrimi et in fabulas traditae crudelitas.

> maître, se fut contenté de désirer la mort, il aurait prononcé sur lui-même le jugement que Jésus-Christ en avait déjà apporté.

Whereas we are told in the text that religion acts to prohibit suicide, Diderot points out in the note that an excess of zeal drives many to scorn this life. The citation of Saint Paul (undoubtedly recorded from memory) is from *Philippians* I, 23, and for Diderot's purposes, Paul's feelings exemplify well the psychology which he describes: "Mihi enim vivere Christus est et mori lucrum quod si vivere in carne, hic mihi fructus operis est, et quod eligam ignoro. Coartor autem e duobus, desiderium habens dissolvi et cum Christo esse, multo magis melius." [17]

In the note on page 39, Diderot declares that

> La hardiesse d'un Egyptien, esprit fort, qui, bravant la doctrine du sacré collège, eût refusé de porter son hommage à des êtres destinés à sa nourriture, et d'adorer un chat, un crocodile, un oignon, eût été pleinement justifié par l'absurdité de cette croyance. Tout dogme qui conduit à des infractions grossières de la loi naturelle ne peut être respecté en sureté de conscience. Lorsque la nature et la morale se récrient contre la voix des ministres, l'obéissance est un crime. Qui niera que le crédule Egyptien, qui, pour donner du secours à son Dieu, eût laissé périr son père, n'eût été un vrai parricide? Si l'on me dit jamais: trahis, vole, pille, tue, c'est ton Dieu qui l'ordonne, je répondrai sans examen: trahir, voler, piller, tuer, sont des crimes; donc Dieu ne me l'ordonne pas. La pureté de la morale peut faire présumer la vérité d'un culte; mais si la morale est corrompue, le culte qui préconise cette dépravation est démontré faux. Quel avantage cette réflexion seule ne donne-t-elle pas au christianisme sur toutes les autres religions! Quelle morale comparable à celle de Jésus-Christ! (*Essai*, note 1, 39)

---

[17] The allusion to Judas' betrayal is based upon *Matthew* XXVI, 20-24:

> Vespere autem facto discumbebat cum duodecim discipulis, et edentibus illis dixit Amen dico vobis quia unus vestrum me traditurus est. Et contristati valde coeperunt singuli dicere Numquid ego sum, domine? At ipse respondens ait Qui intingit mecum manum in parapside, hic me tradet. Filius quidem hominis vadit sicut scriptum est de illo; vae autem homini illi per quem filius hominis traditur: bonum erat ei si natus non fuisset homo ille.

The same opposition we observed in the previous note is constructed here: on one hand, the values of "nature" and their manifestations, "la loi naturelle," "conscience," the concepts of "crime" and "parricide." On the other, dogma, "culte," "les ministres." The opposition culminates in the assertion that "la vérité d'un culte" is judged by the fundamental standards of "la nature" and "la pureté de la morale." The praise of the superiority of Christianity in terms of its moral teachings has to be seen as perfunctory after the reading of the previous note (note 1, page 38), and of course, the exotic camouflage ("le crédule Egyptien....") would be accepted at face value by very few readers. The first sentence of the note is important in itself, for it refers to another case of *disobedience* of religious dogma in favor of higher principles: the actions of the Egyptian "esprit fort" — in contrast to the "crédule Egyptien" — are justified in terms of reason and natural law.

Note 1, page 53 expands Shaftesbury's accusation that those of excessive religious zeal are guilty of distorted self-interest. In the text of page 269 of the *Inquiry:*

> For if the habit be such as to occasion, in every particular, a stricter attention to self good and private interest, it must insensibly diminish the affections towards public good or the interest of society, and introduce a certain narrowness of spirit, which (as some pretend) is peculiarly observable in the devout persons and zealots of almost every religion. (*Inquiry*, 269)

Diderot's note expands the condemnation: "Voilà ce qui constitue proprement la bigoterie; car la vraie piété, qualité presque essentielle à l'héroïsme, étend le cœur et l'esprit" (*Essai*, note 1, p. 53).

Note 1, page 25 is the most sustained addition of several which deal with those who withdraw from society for religious reasons, and therefore betray society in their uselessness. In the text of the *Inquiry*, Shaftesbury reflects upon the possibility of there being, in some remote time or corner of the world, "a certain creature of a more solitary disposition than ever was yet heard of,"

> .... one who had neither mate nor fellow of any kind, nothing of his own likeness, towards which he stood

well-affected or inclined, nor anything without or beyond
himself for which he had the least passion or concern; we
might be apt to say perhaps, without much hesitation,
"that this was doubtless a very melancholy creature, and
that in this unsociable and sullen state he was like to
have a very disconsolate kind of life." But if we were
assured that, notwithstanding all appearances, the creature
enjoyed himself extremely, had a great relish of life, and
was in nothing wanting to his own good, we might
acknowledge, perhaps, "that the creature was no monster,
nor absurdly constituted as to himself." But we should
hardly, after all, be induced to say of him "that he was
a good creature."

Shaftesbury's point has to do with Hobbes's vision of natural man as by no means a communal creature, but one in a constant state of antagonism with his fellows. It is Shaftesbury's belief, however, that man is by definition a social creature (see, for example, *Moralists*, p. 76 f.), and he wishes to show here that man, considered as abstracted from the *system* to which he obviously belongs, cannot be called virtuous or good:

However, should it be urged against us "that such
as he was, the creature was still perfect in himself, and
therefore to be esteemed good; for what had he to do
with others" — in this sense, indeed, we might be forced
to acknowledge "that he was a good creature; if he
could be understood to be absolute and complete in
himself, without any real relation to anything in the
universe besides." For should there be anywhere in nature
a system of which this living creature was to be considered a part, then could he nowise be allowed good; whilst
he plainly appeared to be such a part as made rather to
the harm than good of that system or whole in which
he was included. (*Inquiry*, 244)

But Diderot again chooses not to indicate the relevancy of the question to Hobbes's ideas, and he moves from Shaftesbury's hypothetical hermit to concentrate his attention upon a *particular* kind of "solitaire" — the "solitaire religieux." In the last sentence of his translation of the above paragraph Diderot accuses the "vivant automate" of "solitude et ... inaction," two attributes which disqualify the hermit from being praised as *good*. From this slight addition to Shaftesbury's last sentence develops the long note on page 25.

> Divin anachorète, suspendez un moment la profondeur de vos méditations, et daignez détromper un pauvre *mondain,* et qui se fait gloire de l'être. J'ai des passions, et je serais bien fâché d'en manquer: c'est tres-passionnément que j'aime mon Dieu, mon roi, mon pays, mes parents, mes amis, ma maîtresse et moi-même....

It is here *Diderot* who, from the very first words of the note, focuses the attack upon the lack of contribution made to society by those who take shelter in religious orders: in Shaftesbury's text, there is no mention of religious "solitaires," and the question remains purely conjectural. In the note, it is the "solitude" and "inaction" of the religious which is contrasted with the *bienfaisance* of the "mondain":

> Je fais un grand cas des richesses: j'en ai beaucoup, et j'en désire encore; un homme bienfaisant en a-t-il jamais assez? Qu'il me serait doux de pouvoir animer ce talent qui languit sous mes yeux, unir ces amants que l'indigence retient dans le célibat; venger par mes largesses ce laborieux commerçant des revers de la fortune! Je ne fais chaque jour qu'un ingrat; que ne puis-je en faire un cent! c'est à mon aisance, religieux fanatique, que vous devez le pain que votre quêteur vous apporte....

According to what we have seen in note 1, page 25, note 2, page 29 must be read as *irony*. In the text, Shaftesbury defends a certain self-interest as necessary to self-preservation.

> For if the want of such an affection as that outwards self-preservation be injurious to the species, a creature is ill and unnatural as well through this defect as through the want of any other natural affection. And this no one would doubt to pronounce, if he saw a man who minded not any precipices which lay in his way, nor made any distinction of food, diet, clothing, or whatever else related to his health and being. The same would be averred of one who had a disposition which rendered him averse to any commerce with womankind, and of consequence unfitted him through illness of temper (and not merely

through a defect of constitution) for the propagation of his species or kind. (*Inquiry*, 248)

Diderot's modifications of the last sentence of this passage render the judgment of the hypothetical mysogynist more forceful: "On peut envelopper dans la même *condemnation* quiconque serait *frappé d'aversion* pour le commerce des femmes, et qu'un tempérament dépravé, mais non pas un vice de conformation, rendrait inhabile à la propagation de l'espèce" (*Essai*, 29). The note at the bottom of page 29 is appended to "frappé d'aversion": "On considère ici l'homme dans l'état de pure nature; et il n'est pas question de ces hommes saints qui se sont éloignés du sexe par un esprit de continence, qu'on se garde bien de blâmer. Il est évident que cet endroit ne leur convient en aucune façon; car on ne peut assurément les accuser d'aversion pour les femmes, ou de dépravation dans le tempérament" (*Essai*, note 1, p. 29). It is interesting to note that Diderot protests here that the author of the *Inquiry* is alluding only to a theoretical "natural man," since it was he himself who transformed Shaftesbury's theoretical speculation into a diatribe against religious hermits in note 1, page 25. Accordingly, Diderot's protestations here only make explicit a comparison between Shaftesbury's theoretical example ("....one who had a disposition which rendered him averse to any commerce with womankind ... through illnes of temper") and "ces hommes saints, ceux qui se sont éloignés du sexe par un esprit de continence." "On ne peut assurément les accuser d'aversion pour les femmes" is therefore a tongue-in-cheek comment upon the holy vow of chastity.

Note 1, page 99 is similar in spirit and effect. Diderot makes some modifications in the corresponding text itself: "For whoever is unsociable, and voluntarily shuns society or commerce with the world, must of necessity be morose and ill-natured" (*Inquiry*, 315) becomes "L'homme insociable, ou celui qui s'exile volontairement du monde, et qui, rompant tout commerce avec la société, en abjure entièrement les devoirs, doit être sombre, triste, chagrin, et mal constitué (*Essai*, 99). "En abjure entièrement les devoirs" is an addition which serves to emphasize the treacherousness of a voluntary withdrawal from society, and finally, Diderot is more liberal in the epithets which he applies to one who would turn his back on his duty: "morose and ill-natured" is translated as "sombre, triste, chagrin, et mal constitué." The note is appended to "volontairement."

> Il n'est point ici question de ces pieux solitaires que l'esprit de pénitence, la crainte des dangers du monde, ou quelque autre motif autorisé par les conseils de Jésus-Christ, et par les vues sages de son Eglise, ont confinés dans les déserts. On considère dans tout le cours de cet ouvrage (comme on l'a déjà dit mille fois, quoiqu'il fût toujours aisé de s'en apercevoir) l'homme dans son état naturel, et non sous la loi de grâce.

Diderot's bias on the questions of religious fanaticism should be obvious: he returns particularly to attack the abuses of celibacy and the crimes which are committed in the name of religion. More importantly perhaps, his modifications and additions to Shaftesbury's text indicate considerable interest in the question of virtue as considered independently of adherence to an organized corpus of religious belief. And after all, this separation of ethics and religion is what Diderot's statement in the *Discours préliminaire* had led us to expect: "Le but de cet ouvrage est de montrer que la vertu est *presque* indivisiblement attaché à la connaissance de Dieu" (*Essai*, 12).

III. SOCIAL AND POLITICAL ABUSES.

1. Textual Modifications.

Although those additions and modifications of the *Inquiry* which deal with social injustice and tyranny are fewer in number than those where it is a question of religious abuses, much of the same bitterness in Diderot's attitude is to be found in both cases.

Where there is outrage against the pernicious effects of superstition, there is frequently in Diderot's modifications contiguous evidence of anger against those customs and traditions which corrupt our natural values.

T'is impossible that this can instantly, or without much force and violence, be effaced, or	On a beau les combattre et se tourmenter, ce sont des hôtes intraitables contre lesquels il

struck out of the natural temper, even by means of the most extravagant belief or opinion in the world. (*Inquiry*, 261)

faut recourir aux grands expédients, aux dernières violences. La plus extravagante superstition, l'opinion *nationale* la plus absurde, ne les exclueront jamais parfaitement. (*Essai*, 44)

And he who, being led by false religion or prevailing custom.... (*Inquiry*, 307)

Nous avons fait voir que celui qui, séduit par une religion *absurde,* ou entraîné par la force d'un usage *barbare*.... (*Essai*, 92)

But when, either through superstition or ill custom, there come to be very gross mistakes in the assignment or application of the affection.... (*Inquiry*, 254-55)

Mais lorsque la superstition ou des *coutumes barbares* le précipitent dans de grossières erreurs sur l'emploi de ses affections.... (*Essai*, 38)

In the paragraph following the last above example, on page 38 of the *Essai*:

....Nothing horrid or unnatural, nothing unexemplary, nothing destructive of that natural affection by which the species or society is upheld, may on any account, or through any principle or notion of honour or religion, be at any time affected or prosecuted as a good and proper object of esteem. (*Inquiry*, 255)

Affections na tu re l l e s, fondements de la société, que les *lois sanguinaires d'un point d'honneur* et les principes erronés d'une fausse religion tendent quelque fois à saper. (*Essai*, 38)

The concept of honor and the evils which it condones receive harsh treatment in a previous paragraph:

And thus whatsoever causes a misconception or misapprehension of the worth or value of any object, so as to diminish a due, or raise any undue, irregular or unsocial affection, must necesarily be the

Toute méprise sur la valeur des choses qui tend à détruire quelque affection raisonnable, ou à en produire d'injustes, rend vicieux, et nul motif ne peut excuser cette dépravation. Celui, par exemple, qui, séduit par

occasion of wrong. Thus he who affects or loves a man for the sake of something which is reputed honourable, but which is in reality vicious, is himself vicious and ill. (*Inquiry*, 254)	des vices brillants, a mal placé son estime, est vicieux lui-même. Il est quelquefois aisé de remonter à l'origine de cette corruption *nationale*. (*Essai*, 37)

Modifications found on page 97 of the *Essai* text demonstrate the extent to which Diderot was sensitive to the injustices inherent in the social structure of his country.

It happens with mankind that whilst some are by necessity confined to labour, others are provided with abundance of all things by the pains and labours of inferiors. Now, if among the superior and easy sort there be not something of fit and proper employment raised in the room of what is wanting in common labour and toil.... (*Inquiry*, 313)	Entre les hommes, *l'indigence condamne* les uns au travail, tandis que d'autres, dans une abondance complète, *s'engraissent* de la peine et de *la sueur des premiers*. Si ces opulents ne suppléent par quelque exercice convenable aux fatigues du corps dont ils sont *dispensés par état*.... (*Essai*, 97)

Diderot substitutes "l'indigence condamne les uns au travail" for Shaftesbury's less explicit "some are by necessity confined to labour," and thus underlines a *direct* relationship between poverty and labor — *forced* labor, of a sort, for these people are *condemned* "au travail." The contrast between the two groups, the poor and the rich, is made more salient by Diderot in his replacing "others are provided with abundance of all things by the pains and labour of inferiors" with "tandis que d'autres, dans une abondance complète, s'engraissent de la peine et de la sueur des premiers": Shaftesbury's single phrase becomes two in Diderot's translation. "S'engraissent" adds a vivid, affective touch to the description and subtly presents to the reader the grotesque self-indulgence of those who exploit the poor. "Sueur" likewise contributes to reinforce the wretchedness of the first group. Diderot exchanges "inferiors" for "les premiers" in order to remove any suggestion that the glimpse of class structure which he provides can be justified on the basis of merit, and in order to, we say again, render explicit the direct relationship of exploitation between the rich and those whom "l'indigence condamne au travail."

The addition, in the next sentence, of "dispensés par état," emphasizes the point that the opulence of the rich derives not from their worth or toil, but from social station.

Similar modifications are seen in the paragraph following the above:

We see the enormous growth of luxury in capital cities, such as have been long the seat of empire. We see what improvements are made in vice of every kind where numbers of men are maintained in lazy opulence and wanton plenty. 'Tis otherwise with those who are taken up in due employment, and have been well enured to it from their youth. (*Inquiry*, 313)	A quel excès la débauche n'est-elle pas portée dans ces villes qui sont depuis longtemps le siège de quelque empire! Ces endroits peuplés d'une *infinité* de riches fainéants, et d'une *multitude* d'ignorants illustres, sont plongés dans le dernier débordement. Partout ailleurs, où les hommes *assujettis* au travail dès la jeunesse se font honneur d'exercer dans un âge plus avancé des fonctions utiles à la société, il n'en est pas ainsi. (*Essai*, 97)

In this passage, Diderot emphasizes the prevalence of "luxe" and the extraordinary number of men who contribute nothing to society. The use of "assujettis au travail" instead of a more accurate translation of "taken up in honest and due employment" makes the lot of the workers seem less idyllic and suggests as well that their condition is not entirely theirs by choice.

There are several modifications which deal with tyranny and political injustice. In one instance of relatively minor importance, Diderot expands Shaftesbury's allusion to tyrants as exemplifying those who have a great "need of a supply of social affection." Shaftesbury's "And this the case of tyrants and most unlimited potentates may sufficiently verify and demonstrate" (*Inquiry*, 304) becomes "C'est ce que l'exemple des tyrans, dont le pouvoir, *fondé sur le crime, ne se soutient que par la terreur,* prouve suffisamment" (*Essai*, 88).

A more remarkable series of modifications appears on pages 100-101, where Diderot trenchantly describes the unjust delegation of royal power.

This we see yet more remarkably instanced in persons of the most elevated stations, even in princes, monarchs, and those who seem by their condition to be above ordinary human commerce, and who affect a sort of distant strangeness from the rest of mankind. But their carriage is not the same towards all men. The wiser and better sort, it is true, are often held a distance, as unfit for their intimacy or secret trust. But to compensate this there are others substituted in their room, who though they have the least merit, and are perhaps the most vile and contemptible of men, are sufficient, however to serve the purpose of an imaginary friendship, and can become favourites in form. These are the subjects of humanity in the great. For these we see them often in concern and pain; in these they easily confide; to these they can with pleasure communicate their power and greatness, be open, free, generous, confiding, bountiful, as rejoicing in the action itself; having no intention or aim beyond it; and their interest, in respect of policy, often standing a quite contrary way. But where neither the love of mankind nor the passion for favourites prevails, the tyrannical temper fails not to show itself in its proper colours and to the life, with all the bitterness, cruelty, and mistrust which belong to that solitary and gloomy state of uncommunicative and unfriendly greatness. Nor needs there any particular

Cette passion se manifeste encore bien clairement dans les personnes qui remplissent des postes éminents, dans les princes, dans les monarques, et dans tous ceux que leur condition met au-dessus du commerce ordinaire des hommes, et qui, pour se conserver leurs respects, trouvent à propos de leur dérober leur personne, et de laisser entre les hommages et leur trône une vaste distance. Ils ne sont pas toujours les mêmes: cette affectation se dément dans le domestique. *Ces ténébreux monarques de l'Orient*, ces fiers sultans, se rapprochent de ceux qui les environnent; se livrent et se communiquent: on remarque, à la vérité, qu'ils ne s'adressent pas ordinairement aux plus honnêtes gens; mais qu'importe à la certitude de nos propositions? il suffit que, soumis à la commune loi, ils aient besoin de confidents et d'amis. Que des gens sans aucun mérite, que des esclaves, que des hommes tronqués, que les mortels quelquefois les plus vils et les plus méprisables remplissent ces places d'honneur et soient érigés en favoris, l'énergie de l'affection sociale n'en sera que plus marquée. *C'est pour des monstres que ces princes sont hommes:* ils s'inquiètent pour eux; c'est avec eux qu'ils se déploient, qu'ils sont ouverts, libres, sincères et généreux: *c'est en leur mains qu'ils se plaisent quelquefois à déposer leur sceptre.* Plaisir franc et désintéressé, et même, en bonne politique, la plupart du temps oppose à leurs

proof from history or present time to second this remark. (*Inquiry*, 316)	vrais intérêts, mais toujours au bonheur de leurs sujets. C'est dans ces contrées dis-je, qu'on voit *l'étendard de la tyrannie* arboré dans toutes ses couleurs: le prince devient sombre, méfiant et cruel; ses sujets ressentent l'effet de ces passions horribles, mais nécessaires supports d'une couronne environnée de nuages épais, et couverte d'une obscurité qui la dérobe éternellement aux yeux, à l'accès et à la tendresse. Il est inutile d'appuyer cette réflexion du témoignage de l'histoire. (*Essai*, 100-01)

Just as Diderot suggests the notion of rebelling against corrupt and harmful religious institutions and practices, he does not hesitate to insinuate the idea of political revolt into his translation. Indeed, in a passage we have cited previously, religious and political sedition are suggested simultaneously:

In the other species of creatures around us, there is found generally an exact proportionableness, constancy, and regularity in all their passions and affections; no failure in the care of offspring or of the society to which they are united; no prostitution of themselves; no intemperance or excess of any kind. The smaller creatures, who live as it were in cities (as bees and ants), continue the same train and harmony of life, nor are they ever false to those affections which move them to operate towards their public good. Even those creatures of prey who live the farthest out of society maintain, we see, such a conduct towards one	Toutes les créatures qui nous environnent conservent sans altération l'ordre et la régularité requise dans leurs affections. Jamais d'indolence dans les services qu'elles doivent à leurs petits et à leurs semblables. Lorsque notre voisinage ne les a point dépravées, la prostitution, l'intempérance et les autres excès leur son généralement inconnus. Ces petites créatures qui vivent comme en *république*, les abeilles et les fourmis, suivent, dans toute la durée de leur vie, *les mêmes lois, s'assujettissent au même gouvernement*, et montrent dans leur conduite toujours la même harmonie. Ces affections, qui les encouragent au bien de leur

another as is exactly suitable to the good of their own species. Whilst man, notwithstanding the assistance of religion and the direction of laws, is often found to live in less conformity with Nature, and by means of religion itself is often rendered the more barbarous and inhuman. Marks are set on men; distinctions formed; opinions decreed under the severest penalties; antipathies instilled, and aversions raised in men against the generality of their own species. (*Inquiry*, 291-92).

espèce, ne se dépravent, ne s'affaiblissent, ne s'anéantissent jamais en elles. *Avec* le secours de la religion et sous l'autorité des lois l'homme vit d'une façon moins conforme à sa nature que ne font ces insectes. Ces lois, dont le but est de l'affermir dans la pratique de la justice, sont souvent pour lui des *sujets de révolte;* et cette religion, qui tend à le sanctifier, le rend quelquefois la plus barbare des créatures. On propose des questions, on se chicane sur des mots, on forme des distinctions, on passe aux dénominations odieuses, on proscrit de pures opinions sous des peines sévères: de là naissent les antipathies, les haines et *les séditions.* (*Essai*, 76)

Diderot renders the animal-man comparison political by describing the *republics* of the bees and ants, who, satisfied with this equitable form of government, obey "les mêmes lois" and support this government "dans toute la durée de leur vie." As we have said before, Diderot replaces "*notwithstanding* the assistance of religion and the direction of laws" with "*Avec* le secours de la religion et sous l'autorité des lois," and thus implies that religion and *law* contribute to the corruption of man — since "l'homme vit d'une façon moins conforme à sa nature que ne font ces insectes." In contrast to the political stability of the "petites créatures," man's laws are often for him "des sujets de révolte."

That virtue cannot be crushed by tyranny is indicated by modifications in the text of *Essai*, 55.

For thus a people raised from barbarity or despotic rule, civilised by laws, and made virtuous by the long course of a lawful and just administration, if they chance to fall suddenly under any misgovernment of

S'il arrivait qu'un peuple, arraché au despotisme et à la barbarie, policé par des lois, et devenu vertueux dans le cours d'une administration équitable, retombât brusquement sous un gouvernement arbitraire, *tel*

unjust and arbitrary power, they will on this account be the rather animated to exert a stronger virtue in opposition to such violence and corruption. And even where, by long and continued arts of a prevailing tyranny, such a people are at last totally oppressed the scattered seeds of virtue will for a long time remain alive, even to a second generation, ere the utmost force of misapplied rewards and punishments can bring them to the abject and compliant state of long-accustomed slaves. (*Inquiry*, 272)

que celui des peuples orientaux, sa vertu s'irritant dans les fers, il n'en sera que plus prompt à les secouer et que plus propre à les rompre. Si toutefois la tyrannie et ses artifices viennent à prévaloir, et si ce peuple perd toute liberté, avant qu'une injuste distribution des récompenses et des châtiments lui aient ôté le sentiment de cette injure, avant que l'habitude l'ait fait à sa chaîne, les semences dispersés de sa vertu première pousseront des racines qu'on distinguera jusque dans les générations suivantes. (*Essai*, 55)

The allusion to the ultimately successful rebellion of an oppressed people against despotic rule is Diderot's. In the last sentence of this passage, the order of Shaftesbury's sentence is adjusted so that the sentence might end, not with a description of the victory of tyranny, but with praise of the noble strength of virtue.

On page 74 of the *Essai*, Diderot adds a long passage in praise of the courage of those who overthrow unjust political systems.

And of all other creatures, man is in this sense the most formidable, since if he thinks it just and exemplary, he may, possibly in his own or in his country's cause, revenge an injury on any one living, and by throwing away his own life (if he be resolute to that degree) is almost certain master of another's, however strongly guarded. Examples of this nature have often served to restrain those in power from using it to the utmost extent, and urging their inferiors to extremity (*Inquiry*, 290.)

De tous les êtres vivants, l'homme est le plus formidable en ce sens. Lorsqu'il s'agira de sa propre cause ou de celle de son pays, il n'y a personne dont il ne puisse tirer une vengeance, qu'il regardera comme équitable et exemplaire; et s'il est assez *intrépide* pour sacrifier sa vie, il est maître de celle d'un autre, quelque bien gardé qu'il puisse etre. *Dans ces républiques de l'antiquité, où les peuples nés libres ont été quelquefois subjugués par l'ambition d'un citoyen, on a vu des exemples de ce courage, et des usurpateurs punis, malgré leur vigilance, des cruautés qu'ils*

> *avaient exercées; on a vu des hommes généreux tromper toutes les précautions possibles, et assurer par la mort des tyrans le salut et la liberté de leur patrie.* (*Essai,* 74)

It is easy to see where Diderot's sympathies lie. He first substitutes an affective adjective, "intrépide," for Shaftesbury's modest "if he be resolute to that degree," and this first word of praise is echoed in "des exemples de ce courage" and "hommes généreux." Obviously, what is most important to note here is the expanded last sentence of Diderot's paragraph, where he drives home the point of the courageous behavior of those who pierce the security surrounding political leaders and slay the tyrant who has unjustly usurped power. This modification of Shaftesbury's text is surely one of the most bold to come from Diderot's hand.

2. Footnote Additions.

Note 1, page 74 is Diderot's addition to his own modifications, and it increases the force of the point.

> J'ai cru devoir rectifier ici la pensée de M... S..., qui nomme hardiment et conséquemment aux préjugés de sa nation, vertu, courage, héroïsme, le meurtre d'un tyran en général. Car si ce tyran est roi par sa naissance, ou par le choix libre des peuples, il est de principe parmi nous, que, se portât-il aux plus étranges excès, c'est toujours un crime horrible que d'attenter à sa vie. La Sorbonne l'a décidé en 1626. Les premiers fidèles n'ont pas cru qu'il leur fût permis de conspirer contre leurs persécuteurs, Néron, Dèce, Dioclétien, etc., et saint Paul a dit expressément: *Obedite praepositis vestris etiam discolis, et subjacete eis.* (*Essai*, note 1, 74)

The first sentence of the note appears to be, in the eyes of the reader, an attempt to disclaim responsibility for the bold remarks in "Shaftesbury's" text. But since we know that the remarks in question are the work of the translator, the tone of the entire note is insincere; and indeed, to suggest that regicide is out of the question because the Sorbonne has judged it to be so is an exercise in irony.[18]

Note 1, page 100 is an expanded reflection on the transfer of political power into the hands of unscrupulous royal favorites.

> .... Il n'est pas rare de voir un valet de sérail passer de dignités en dignités jusqu'à celle de vizir; devenir le fléau des peuples, et finir par une mort tragique dans ces révoltes ordinaires à Constantinople, où le ministre est aussi lâchement abandonné par son maître, et sacrifié à la fureur des rebelles, qu'il en fut aveuglément élevè a une place où l'on ne devrait jamais faire asseoir que le mérite et la vertu. (*Essai*, note 1, 100)

Note 2, page 76 is in part taken from Locke's *Essay*, Book I, chapter ii, section 9, the chapter entitled "No Innate Principles" [19] — the same text, in fact, which constitutes the source of note 1, page 45. Locke's passage reads:

> But I cannot see how any men should ever transgress those moral rules, with confidence and serenity, were they innate, and stamped upon their minds.... Have there not been whole nations, and those of the most civilized people, amongst whom the exposing their children, and leaving them in the fields to perish by want or wild beasts has been the practice; as little condemned or scrupuled as the begetting them? Do they not still, in some countries, put them into the same graves with their mothers, if they die in childbirth; or despatch them, if a pretended astrologer declares them to have unhappy stars? And are there not places where, at a certain age, they will or expose their parents, without any remorse at all? In a

---

[18] See Dorothy Schlegel, *Shaftesbury and The French Deists*, p. 50. Mrs. Schlegel calls note 1, page 74 an example of *reductio ad absurdum*, and accurately states that "In a note purporting to disagree with Shaftesbury's statements praising tyrannicide, Diderot asserts that to make an attempt on the life of a king is a horrible crime for the reason that the Sorbonne had decided against it in 1626. The citation of the faithful and of Saint Paul as additional authorities who had opposed regicide are inserted merely as an ironical afterthought and for extra protection." But Mrs. Schlegel apparently did not notice that the statements in the *text* of page 74 were not Shaftesbury's but Diderot's.

[19] Venturi seems uncertain as to the source of this note; see *La Jeunesse*, p. 355.

part of Asia, the sick, when their case comes to be thought desperate, are carried out and laid on the earth before they are dead; and left there, exposed to wind and weather, to perish without assistance or pity. It is familiar among the Mingrelians, a people professing Christianity, to bury their children alive without scrupule. There are places where they eat their own children. The Caribes were wont to geld their children, on purpose to fat and eat them. And Garcilasso de la Vega tells us of a people in Peru which were wont to fat and eat the children they got on their female captives, whom they kept as concubines for that purpose, and when they were past breeding, the mothers themselves were killed too and eaten.

Diderot's note is appended to a passage which we have already examined (see "J'oserais assurer qu'il est presque impossible de trouver sur la terre une société d'hommes qui se gouvernent par des principes humains," *Essai*, 76), and Diderot here extends his condemnation of human conduct.

> Qui prendra la peine de lire avec soin l'histoire du genre humain, et d'examiner d'un œil indifférent la conduite des peuples de la terre, se convaincra lui-même, que, excepté les devoirs qui sont absolument nécessaires à la conservation de la société humaine (qui ne sont même que trop souvent violés par des sociétés entières à l'égard des autres sociétés), on ne saurait nommer aucun principe de morale, ni imaginer aucune règle de vertu, qui dans quelque endroit du monde ne soit méprisé, ou contredite par la pratique générale de quelques sociétés entières, qui sont gouvernées par des maximes, et dirigées par des règles tout à fait opposées à celles de quelque autre société.

Diderot then inserts the documentation from Locke (without acknowledging his source), after which he extends the field of vision to include contemporary European culture: "Les usages, les religions et les gouvernements divers qui partagent l'Europe, nous fourniraient une multitude d'actions moins barbares en apparence, mais aussi déraisonables au fond, et peut-être plus dangereuses dans les conséquences." Note 2, page 76 is then parallel in form to note 1, page 76, where it is likewise a question of pointing out the barbarism of exotic cultures in order to suggest that European — or French — culture offers no improvement. In the second note Diderot gives us a description of human corruption, despite the fact that he has already shown us that he is committed to the theoretical existence of objective values.

IV. Virtue

It is upon the subject of virtue that Diderot's agreement with Shaftesbury is most manifest, insofar as his translation indicates less significant deviation from the nature of the original in this area than was the case where religious and political institutions were concerned. The various additions and modifications which we have classified under the general rubric "virtue" demonstrate, with some exceptions, less Diderot's wish to drastically modify Shaftesbury's argument than his interest in supporting or reinforcing it with his own interpretations.

A word should be said here about Diderot's translation of the title *An Inquiry Concerning Virtue or Merit* as *Essai sur le mérite et la vertu*. Diderot translates "Inquiry" as "Essai" throughout, and he takes little care in the *Essai* to distinguish between the words "virtue" and "merit." For example, on page 23 of the *Essai* Diderot renders "virtue and merit" as "vertu" (compare *Inquiry*, 242). On page 30, "goodness" is rendered as "le mérite"; on page 29, "virtue" becomes "mérite"; on page 32, "virtue or merit" is again translated as simply "vertu," but on page 38 "worth and virtue" is translated as "le mérite *ou* la vertu" (my italics). This brief sample of evidence would suggest that the changes that Diderot makes when "virtue," "merit," "virtue or merit," and so forth appear in Shaftesbury's text are without philosophical or even stylistic import.

It might be instructive as well to ask why Diderot refers, in the *Discours préliminaire,* to "vertu *morale*" ("il n'est question dans cet Essai que de la vertu morale; de cette vertu que les saints Pères mêmes ont accordée à quelques philosophes païens; vertu, que le culte qu'ils professaient, soit de cœur, soit en apparence, tendait de détruire de fond en comble, bien loin d'en être inséparable ...."; *Essai,* 12). Shaftesbury himself distinguishes "*moral* virtue" as virtue considered independent of a religious context.

> Little were you aware that the cruel enemy opposed to virtue should be religion itself! But you will call to mind that even innocently, and without any treacherous design, virtue is often treated so by those who would magnify to the utmost the corruption of man's heart; and in exposing, as they pretend, the falsehood of human virtue, think to extol religion. How many religious authors, how many sacred orators, turn all their edge this way, and strike at *moral virtue* as a kind of stepdame, or rival to religion! (*Moralists*, 46)

Hence for Shaftesbury, and for Diderot, who frequently in the *Essai* substitutes "vertu morale" for "virtue," "moral virtue" seems to possess the sense of "natural virtue," the product not of religious teaching, but of man's own efforts and ideals, and in contrast to a pessimistic view of man and his culture as essentially evil. Once again then, Diderot has gone beyond what Shaftesbury presents in the *Inquiry* in order to render more explicit a distinction between *virtue* and religious belief and teaching.

1. *Virtue and Happiness.*

A. Textual Modifications.

On page 77 of the *Essai* there is to be found a curious addition which consists of a long paragraph entirely of Diderot's hand. Therein, despite the fact that a main goal of the *Essai* has avowedly been to show that man is capable of virtue, and thereby of happiness in this world, Diderot reflects in fact upon the poverty of temporal happines:

> Au reste, lorsque nous assurons que l'économie des affections sociales fait le bonheur temporel, c'est autant que la créature peut être heureuse dans ce monde. Nous ne prétendons rien prouver de contraire à l'expérience: or elle ne nous apprend que trop bien que les orages passagers, qui troublent l'homme le plus heureux, sont pour le moins aussi fréquents que les fautes légères qui échappent à l'homme le plus juste. Ajoutez à cela ces élans

> continuels vers l'éternité, ces mouvements d'une âme qui sent le vide de son état actuel, mouvements d'autant plus vifs que la ferveur est grande: d'où l'on peut conclure, sans aller plus loin, que, s'il est vrai qu'il y ait du bonheur attaché à la pratique des vertus, comme nous le démontrerons, il ne l'est pas moins que la créature ne peut jouir d'une félicité proportionnée à ses désirs, d'un bonheur qui la remplisse, d'un repos immuable, que dans le sein de la Divinité.

It could of course be that Diderot is simply supplying another testimony of religious orthodoxy, since this paragraph follows rather closely a passage which contains rebukes of religious and political institutions (*Essai*, 76). Nevertheless, in my view, this passage carries a sincere ring of despair, disillusionment, and world-weariness, and is similar to other such statements which appear from time to time throughout Diderot's work, particularly in his correspondence.[20] If the lack of enthusiasm for the ultimate value of terrestial happiness is in good faith, it is to a large degree corroborated by the substance of note 1, page 60.

B. Additions.

Note 1, page 60 of the *Essai* is appended to a passage in which Shaftesbury argues that "A person believing rewards or retributions

---

[20] See for example, the letter to Falconet dated February 15, 1766: "Ne me détachez pas de la meilleure partie de mon bonheur. Celui que je me promets, est presque toujours plus grand que celui dont je jouis, ce n'est pas chez moi, c'est dans mon château en Espagne que je suis pleinement satisfait. Aussi quelque événement le renverse-t-il? Je me hâte bien vite d'en rebâtir un autre. C'est là que je me sauve des fâcheux, des méchants, des importuns, des envieux; c'est là que j'habite les deux tiers de ma vie" (*Le Pour et le Contre,* ed. Yves Benot, Paris, 1966, p. 74). And:

> Je vous ferai une fable. Le bonheur habita une fois sur la terre, mais le bonheur vrai; le bonheur en propre personne. Soit que ce pauvre séjour ne fut pas fait pour lui, soit qu'il soit léger de sa nature, soit qu'il ne puisse demeurer en place, il s'en alla je ne sais où, au ciel peut-être ou sous la tombe. Mais en s'en allant, il laissa ses vêtemens. La peine qui marchoit toujours sur ses pas, et qui ne trouvoit personne qui voulut l'héberger, s'en saisit; et c'est elle qui se présente sans cesse à nous sous vêtement du plaisir. La peine sous le vêtement du plaisir, c'est moi pour vous, c'est vous pour moi; c'est tout ce qui s'offre à nous sur la terre et qui nous séduit. ("Fragment sans date," in *Lettres à Sophie Volland,* ed. Andre Badelon, Paris, 1930, III, 281).

in another life, must believe them annexed to real goodness and merit, real villainy and baseness, and not to any accidental qualities of circumstances, in which respect they cannot properly be styled rewards or punishments, but capricious distributions of happiness or unhappiness to creatures" (*Inquiry*, 276). To believe that justice will come in a future life will fortify that man who might feel that virtue is "naturally an enemy to happiness in life." But Shaftesbury continues, "This ... is an opinion which cannot be supposed consistent with sound theism...." Diderot affixes his note here; but Shaftesbury goes on to assert that the man who believes intelligence and order to reign generally in Nature must therefore believe "virtue to be naturally good and advantageous." Diderot's reflection however reveals less secure belief:

> Si la vertu a des avantages actuels, *toutefois il en coûte pour être vertueux;* si l'état de l'honnête homme, ici-bas, n'est pas déplorable, il s'en faut bien que sa félicité soit complète: il lui reste toujours des désirs; et ces désirs, preuves incontestables de *l'insuffisance de sa récompense actuelle,* ne conspirent-ils pas avec la révélation qu'il est près d'admettre, pour l'assurer d'une vie à venir?

Still, if we believe that virtue brings us only grief, will we not be led to conclude that there is no God?

> Mais si l'on supposait, au contraire, que l'honnête homme ne peut être que malheureux en ce monde, et que la félicité temporelle est incompatible avec la vertu, l'économie singulière qui régnerait dans l'univers ne le porterait-elle pas à se méfier de l'ordre qui régnera dans l'autre vie? *Décrier la vertu n'est-ce donc pas prêter main-forte à l'athéisme? Amplifier les désordres apparents de la nature,* n'est-ce pas ébranler l'existence d'un Dieu, sans fortifier la croyance d'une vie à venir?

Venturi claims that this note "ne se retrouve pas littéralement dans Shaftesbury, bien qu'elle soit une exposition sommaire des idées de celui-ci" (*La Jeunesse,* 350); but the note is very clearly Diderot's reworking of pages 57-59 of *The Moralists,* which I shall quote at length.

"'Tis true, though the appearances hold ever so strongly against virtue, and in favour of vice, the objection which arises hence against a Deity may be easily removed, and all set right again on the supposal of a future state.... Being once convinced of order and a providence as to things present, one may soon, perhaps, be satisfied even of a future state. For if virtue be to itself no small reward, and vice in a great measure its own punishment, we have a solid ground to go upon....

But as many as are the difficulties which Virtue has to encounter in this world, her force is yet superior. Exposed as she is here, she is not yet however abandoned or left miserable.... Her present portion is sufficient to show Providence already engaged on her side....

.... A providence must be proved from what we see of order in things present. We must contend for order; and in this part chiefly, where virtue is concerned, all must not be referred to a hereafter. For a disordered state, in which all present care of things is given up, vice uncontrolled, and virtue neglected, represents a very chaos, and reduces us to the beloved atoms, chance, and confusion of the atheists.

.... What therefore can be worse done in the cause of a Deity than to magnify disorder, and exaggerate (as some zealous people do) the misfortunes of virtue, so far as to render it an unhappy choice with respect to this world?... Nor can it be thought sincerely that any man, by having the most elevated opinion of virtue, and of the happiness it creates, was ever the less inclined to the belief of a future state.'"

Diderot seems to lack the assurance of Shaftesbury where the existence of ordained moral order is concerned ("Amplifier les désordres *apparents* de la nature....") and where it is a question of the value of the correlation happiness-virtue in this life ("preuves incontestables de l'insuffisance de sa récompense actuelle"). Nor does the achievement of virtue come without sacrifice and effort: "il en coûte pour être vertueux." Indeed, for Diderot, what seems to possess the greatest force as an argument for "une vie à venir" is not the "present portion" of virtue, but rather, as we have seen in the addition on page 77, man's *desire*, his unsatisfied longing for complete fulfillment and perfection, "ces élans continuels vers l'éternité."

Conversely, if Diderot cannot proclaim that happiness accompanies virtue with overwhelming consistency in this life, he maintains with greater force that the evil man receives his just deserts. Note 1, page 91 develops from Shaftesbury's assertion that "There scarcely is, or can be, any creature whom consciousness of villainy, as such merely, does not at all offend; nor anything opprobrious or heinously imputable move or affect" (*Inquiry*, 306; Diderot: "Il n'y a peut-être pas une créature parfaitement insensible à la honte des crimes qu'elle a commis; pas une qui se reconnaisse *intérieurement* digne de l'opprobre et de la haine de ses semblables...."). The note consists of an imprecise citation of two verses of Louis Racine's *Poëme sur la Religion* (1742): Diderot's note reads "Le crime ... est le premier bourreau, / Qui dans un sein coupable enfonce la couteau." The lines are extracted from the following context:

>C'est pour moi que je vis, je ne dois rien qu'à moi.
>La vertu n'est qu'un nom, mon plaisir est ma loi.
>Ainsi parle l'Impie, & lui-même est l'esclave
>De la foi, de l'honneur, de la vertu qu'il brave:
>Dans ses honteux plaisirs s'il cherche à se cacher,
>Un eternel témoin les lui vient reprocher:
>Son juge est dans son cœur, tribunal où réside
>Le censeur de l'ingrat, du Traître, du perfide.
>Si par ses noirs complots nous sommes outragés,
>De près suivra la peine, & nous serons vengés.
>De ses remords secrets triste & lente victime,
>Jamais un criminel ne s'absout de son crime.
>Sous des lambris dorés le pâle ambitieux
>Vers le Ciel, sa terreur, n'ose lever les yeux.
>Suspendu sur sa tête, un glaive redoutable
>Rend fades tous les mets dont on couvre sa table.
>Le cruel repentir est le premier boureau [sic]
>Qui dans un sein coupable enfonce le couteau.
>(Chant I, 371-386)

The fact that Diderot does not accurately cite Racine is an indication that the passage was probably well enough known to be quoted from memory. The source itself is interesting when one considers that Chant I of *La Religion* begins with the verse "La Raison dans mes vers conduit l'homme à la foi," and that in the preface the author declares: "J'examine la foiblesse de mon esprit, & je reconnois que ma Raison ne doit pas être ma seule lumière. J'examine mon cœur, & je reconnois que la morale Chrétienne est conforme à ses besoins. J'embrasse avec joie une Religion aussi aimable que respectable." With respect to the verses cited by Diderot in the *Essai* however, it appears that he and Racine agree that an evil man in reality does not perpetrate evil with impunity, for the force of conscience cannot be stifled in even the darkest of hearts.

History moreover proves that wrongdoing brings grief upon the head of the miscreant. Note 1, page 118 grows out of Shaftesbury's reflection to the effect that "Hence it appears that the greatest of miseries accompanies that state which is consequent to the loss of natural affection; and that to have those horrid, monstrous, and unnatural affections is to be miserable in the highest degree" (*Inquiry*, 336). I quote the note only in part here:

> Je ne crois pas qu'on trouve jamais l'histoire en contradiction avec cette conclusion de notre philosophe. Ouvrons les *Annales* de Tacite, ces fastes de la méchanceté des hommes; parcourons le règne de Tibere, de Claude, de Caligula, de Néron, de Galba, et le destin rapide de tous leurs courtisans; et renonçons à nos principes, si dans la foule de ces scélerats insignes qui déchirent les entrailles de leur patrie, et dont les fureurs ont ensanglanté toutes les pages, toutes les lignes de cette histoire, nous rencontrons un heureux.

Nevertheless, Diderot already in the *Essai* gives evidence of fascination with the *monstre*, the magnificently evil being.

> On trouve dans la Vie de Caligula des exemples presque uniques de cette passion ["cette fierté tyrannique qui en veut à toute liberté, et qui regarde toute prospérité d'un œil chagrin et jaloux"; *Essai*, 115]. Jaloux d'immortaliser sa mémoire par de vastes calamités, il enviait à Auguste le bonheur d'une armée entière massacrée sous son règne; et à Tibère, la chute de l'Amphithéâtre sous lequel cinquante mille âmes périrent. S'étant avisé, à la représentation de quelque pièce de théâtre, d'applaudir mal à propos un acteur que le peuple siffla: Ah! si tous ces gosiers, s'écria-t-il, étaient sous une tête!... Voilà ce qu'on pourrait appeler le sublime de la cruauté. (*Essai*, 115 note)

A passage which begins as a condemnation of evil ends on a note of wonder and admiration of a supremely evil man.

2. The Question of Objective Values: Note 2, page 33, and Note 1, page 119.

Note 2, page 33 of the *Essai* is interesting and significant as regards the early formulation of Diderot's esthetic theory.[21] To be sure, the note develops from Shaftesbury's point on the question of objective values, both ethical and esthetic: "The mind, which is spectator or auditor of other minds, cannot be without its eye and ear, so as to discern proportion, distinguish sound, and scan each sentiment or though which comes before it. It can let nothing escape its censure.... So that to deny the common and natural sense of a sublime and beautiful in things, will appear an affectation merely, to any one who considers duly of this affair" (*Inquiry*, 251-52). The vocabularies of both Shaftesbury and Diderot demonstrate the extent to which they see ethical and esthetic judgments as interrelated and similar. But Diderot's note moves finally to the level of values in esthetics, and to the question of whether beauty exists objectively.

The first part of the note is adapted in great part, as Franco Venturi has indicated (*La Jeunesse*, p. 350), from *Miscellaneous Reflections* (ed. Robertson, II, 174-75).

> S'il n'y a ni beau, ni grand, ni sublime dans les choses, que deviennent l'amour, la gloire, l'ambition, la valeur? À quoi bon admirer un poème ou un tableau, un palais ou un jardin, une belle taille ou un beau visage? Dans ce système flégmatique, l'héroïsme est une extravagance. On ne fera pas plus de quartier aux muses. Le prince des poètes ne sera qu'un écrivain suffisamment insipide. Mais cette philosophie meurtrière se dément à chaque moment; et ce poète, qui a employé tous les charmes de son art pour décrier ceux de la nature, s'abandonne plus que personne aux transports, aux ravissements et à l'enthousiasme; et, à en juger par la vivacité de ses descriptions, qui que

---

[21] See L. G. Crocker, *Two Diderot Studies, Ethics and Esthetics*, Baltimore, Johns Hopkins Press, 1952, p. 62 and p. 116.

ce soit ne fut plus sensible que lui aux beautés de l'univers. On pourrait dire que sa poésie fait plus de tort à l'hypothèse des atomes que tous ses raisonnements ne lui donnent de vraisemblance. Ecoutons-le chanter un moment:

Alma Venus, coeli subter labentia signa
Quae mare navigerum, quae terras frugiferenteis
Concelebras.... (LUCRET. De rerum nat. lib. I, v. 1)
Quae quoniam rerum naturam sola gubernas,
Nec sine te quidquam dias in luminas oras
Exoritur, neque fit laetum, neque amabile quodquam;
Te sociam studeo scribundis versibus esse.
(Ib. ibid., v. 22)

Quand on a senti toute la grâce de cette invocation, tout ce qu'on peut alléguer contre la beauté ne doit faire qu'une impression bien légère.
Et ailleurs:

Belli fera moenera Mavors
Armipotens regit, in gremium qui saepe tuum se
Rejicit, aeterno devictus volnere amoris....
Pascit amoro avidos, inhians in te, Dea, visus;
Eque tuo pendet resupini spiritus ore,
Hunc tu, Diva, tuo recubantem corpore sancto
Circumfusa super, suaveis ex ore loquelas
Funde.
(LUCRET. *De rerum nat.*, lib. I, v. 34)

Shaftesbury's text is as follows:

> Slender would be the enjoyments of the lover, the ambitious man, the warrior, or the virtuoso . . . , if in the beauties which they admire and passionately pursue there were no reference or regard to any hgher majesty or grandeur than what simply results from the particular objects of their pursuit. I know not, in reality, what we should do to find a seasoning to most of our pleasures in life, were it not for the taste or relish which to this particular passion, and the conceit or imagination which supports it. Without this, we could not so much as admire a poem or a picture; a garden or a palace; a charming shape or a fair face. Love itself would appear the lowest thing in Nature when thus anticipated, and treated according to the antienthusiastic poet's method: —
>
> Et jacere humorem collectum in corpora quaeque
>
> How heroism or magnanimity must stand in this hypothesis is easy to imagine. The Muses themselves must make

a very indifferent figure in this philosophical draught. Even the prince of poets would prove a most insipid writer if he were thus reduced. Nor could there, according to this scheme, be yet a place of honour left even for our Latin poet, the great disciple of this un-polite philosophy, who dares with so little equity employ the Muses' art in favour of such a system. But in spite of his philosophy he everywhere gives way to admiration and rapturous views of Nature. He is transported with the several beauties of the world, even whilst he arraigns the order of it, and destroys the principle of beauty from whence in ancient languages the world itself was named.

But what follows in the second part of Diderot's note develops, in dialogue form at first, as a conflict between Diderot's position and an attitude represented by Shaftesbury himself in certain pages of *The Moralists*.

> *Je conviens que ces vers sont d'une grande beauté,* dira-t-on. Il y a quelque chose de beau? *Sans doute, mais ce n'est pas dans la chose décrite, c'est dans la description: il n'est point de monstre odieux qui, par l'art imité, ne puisse plaire aux yeux; quelque difforme que soit un être (si toutefois il y a difformité réelle), il plaira pourvu qu'il soit bien représenté. Mais cette représentation qui me ravit ne suppose aucune beauté dans la chose: ce que j'admire, c'est la conformité de l'objet et de la peinture. La peinture est belle, mais l'objet n'est ni beau ni laid.* (Diderots's italics)

The argument that beauty truly resides not in things but in art, not in forms but in the forming, is offered in *The Moralists* by Theocles: [22]

---

[22] Shaftesbury's attitude partakes of a long tradition; see, for example, Plotinus, *Enneads*, V, viii:
> Suppose two blocks of stone lying side by side, one unpatterned, quite untouched by art, the other wrought into the statue of some god or man, Grace or Muse — a creation in which the sculptor's art has concentrated every loveliness.
> Now the stone thus wrought by the artist's hand to beauty of form is beautiful not as stone — for so the crude block would be as pleasant — but in virtue of the form imposed on it by art... The beauty, therefore, exists in a far higher state in the art; that original beauty is not transferred; what comes over is a derivative and a minor, and even that appears in the statue only in so far as the stone yielded to the art.

> Thus then, said Theocles (smiling), whatever passion you may have for other beauties, I know, good Philocles, you are no such admirer of wealth in any kind as to allow much beauty to it, especially in a rude heap or mass. But in medals, coins, embossed work, statues, and well-fabricated pieces, of wratever sort, you can discover beauty and admire the kind. True, said I, but not for the metal's sake. 'Tis not then the metal or matter which is beautiful with you? No. But the art? Certainly. The art then is the beauty? Right. And the art is that which beautifies? The same. So that the beautifying, not the beautified, is the really beautiful? It seems so. For that which is beautified, is beautiful only by the accession of something beautifying, and by the recess or withdrawing of the same, it ceases to be beautiful? Be it. In respect of bodies therefore, beauty comes and goes? So we see. Nor is the body itself any cause either of its coming or staying? None. No that there is no principle of beauty in body? None at all.... Must not that, therefore, which means and intends for it, regulates and orders it, be the principle of beauty to it? Of necessity. And what must that be? Mind, I suppose, for what can it be else? —
> .... All which is void of mind is horrid, and matter formless is deformity itself. (*Moralists*, 131-132)

Diderot begins his response to this position taken by his "adversary" by asking "ce qu'on entend par un *monstre*": "Si l'on désigne par ce terme un composé de parties rassemblées au hasard, sans liaison, sans ordre, sans harmonie, sans proportion, j'ose assurer que la représentation de cet être ne sera pas moins choquante que l'être lui-même." If a painter, "dans le dessein d'une tête," takes such liberties as placing "les dents au-dessous du menton, les yeux à l'occiput et la langue au front," no amount of artistic skill can render such a composition beautiful: "la délicatesse du pinceau ne nous fera jamais admirer cette figure." If we mean by *monstre* "Un être qui ressemble à quelque chose, tel que la sirène, l'hippogriffe, le faune, le sphinx, la chimère et les dragons ailés," we should recognize that these *monstres* "n'ont rien d'absurde dans leur conformation;[23] [et]que, quoiqu'ils

---

[23] On other uses of "conformation," see for example, *Essai*, 23, where "conformation" translates "compass of his make" (*Inquiry*, 243); *Essai*, 25, where "conformation" is used twice, once as the equivalent of "structure,"

n'existent pas dans la nature, ils n'ont rien de contradictoire aux idées de liaison, d'harmonie, d'ordre et de proportion[.] Il y a plus, n'est-il pas constant qu'aussitôt que ces figures pécheront contre ces idées, elles cesseront d'être belles?" But who has determined how sphinxes, sirens, and dragons should be represented? "Puisque ces êtres n'existent point dans la nature, qui est-ce qui a déterminé la longueur de la queue de la sirène, l'étendue des ailes du dragon, la position des yeux du sphinx et la grosseur de la cuisse velue et du pied fourchu des sylvains? *car ces choses ne sont pas arbitraires*" (my italics). One could answer simply that for no reason in particular — "sans fondement" — we insist that representations of these beings observe certain rules of *relationship* which we see in creatures that *do* exist, "et que c'est encore ici la ressemblance qui produit notre admiration." Yet this is precisely the question: is it reason or caprice which causes us to demand of artists the observation of "la loi des êtres réels" in the representation of imaginary beings? For Diderot, there is an objective criterion: "dans l'univers, les devoirs à remplir déterminent l'organisation." [24] The physical structure of any being is determined by its needs, and "l'organisation est plus ou moins parfaite, selon le plus ou le moins de facilité que l'automate en reçoit pour vaquer à ses fonctions." And that individual whose physical form is most satisfying to his needs is the most *beautiful:* "Car qu'est-ce qu'un bel homme, si ce n'est celui dont les membres bien proportionnés conspirent de la façon la plus avantageuse à l'accomplissement des fonctions animales?" The beauty of any creature then is in direct proportion to the perfection of *l'organisation:* that which is most functional — most practical, most useful — is also most beautiful: beauty and utility coincide. Hence, insists Diderot, beauty is not "arbitraire"; it exists *in* beautiful forms of nature, in material forms: beauty does not exist exclusively in the beautifying nor in the conformity

---

and again in place of "proportions" (*Inquiry*, 245). On page 26 of the *Essai*, "conformation" replaces "structure" (*Inquiry*, 245). On page 29 "conformation" translates "constitution" (*Inquiry*, 248); likewise on page 30 (*Inquiry*, 249). A somewhat different use appears on page 44 where "conformation" translates "frame and order of our bodies" (*Inquiry*, 260).

[24] See use of this word, page 38 of the *Essai:* "l'organisation" translates "formation and structure" (*Inquiry*, 314).

between "l'objet et la peinture." Now of course, as has already been suggested, the perfect *organisation* embodies "les idées de liaison, d'harmonie, d'ordre et de proportion." That *organisation* which is perfecly practical is beautiful because it is at the same time formed according to the principles of *ordre, harmonie, proportion*. Any object in nature which does not conform to these principles can never be rendered beautiful through art; any object which does in fact conform to these objective constants will be beautiful (and useful) exclusive of art.

Shaftesbury too attests to a relationship between le *beau* and l'*utile;* in the *Miscellaneous Reflections,* for example:

> The same features which make deformity create incommodiousness and disease. And the same shapes and proportions which make beauty afford advantage by adapting to activity and use. Even in the imitative or designing arts... the truth or beauty of every figure or statue is measured from the perfection of Nature in her just adapting of every limb and proportion to the activity, strength, dexterity, life and vigour of the particular species or animal designed. (*Miscellaneous Reflections,* ed. Robertson, II, 267)

However, what is most noticeably not present in Diderot's argument when it is contrasted with Shaftesbury's idea is the allusion to intelligence — to the "beautifying" Mind. [25] In Diderot's note we are told that certain forms are beautiful *in themselves,* but we are not treated to a glorification of the forming powers of divine intelligence: beauty objectively exists, maintains Diderot, independently of any higher reality. It is not surprising therefore that Diderot begins his polemic with an allusion to Lucretius, the poet who praises the beauty of nature in and for itself. The conclusion at which Diderot arrives in this note to the *Essai* already then suggests the position taken in *Recherches philosophiques sur l'origine et la nature du beau* of some seven years later: "Le

---

[25] As Bernard Bosanquet states: "Shaftesbury ... stands, so far as aesthetic is concerned, on the same metaphysical ground of the Christian intelligence, believing beauty to be an expression of the divine life of the world, which he contrasts with dead matter in a way too much akin to Plotinus, and is therefore unable to find an explanation for ugliness or evil" (*A History of Aesthetic,* New York, Meridian Books, 1961, p. 177).

beau n'est pas toujours l'ouvrage d'une cause intelligente: le mouvement établit souvent, soit dans un être considéré solitairement, soit entre plusieurs êtres comparés entre eux, une multitude prodigieuse de rapports surprenants. Les cabinets d'histoire naturelle en offrent un grand nombre d'exemples. Les rapports sont alors des résultats de combinaisons fortuites, du moins par rapport à nous" (in *Œuvres esthétiques,* ed. Paul Vernière, Classiques Garnier, 1959, p. 435).

Note 1, page 119 is (as Venturi has shown) a reformulation of *Miscellaneous Reflections,* 275-76. Diderot nevertheless characteristically transforms Shaftesbury's direct statement into a dialogue between himself and the Pyrrhonist, and his argument is one that he will use later against the Pyrrhoniens,[26] namely, that their protests against the defense of objective values are only insincere and futile *jeux métaphysiques:* "... le pyrrhonien même laisse ces subtilités à la porte de l'école, et suit le train commun. S'il perd au jeu, il paie comme si c'était lui qui eût perdu. Sans avoir plus de foi à ses raisonnements que lui, je tiendrai donc pour assuré que *j'étais,* que *je suis,* et que *je continuerai d'être moi;* et conséquemment qu'il est possible de me démontrer *quel je dois être* pour mon bonheur" (Diderot's italics).

3. The Moral Sense: "*cœur,*" "*sentiment intérieur,*" "*conscience.*"

It is also of consequence for Diderot's later theory, and for eighteenth-century esthetic and ethical theory in general, to note that in the *Essai* Diderot very often uses the words "cœur" and

---

[26] See *La Promenade du sceptique,* A.-T. I, 216: "La première compagnie, dont l'origine remonte bien avant dans l'antiquité, est composée de gens qui vous disent nettement ... que tout ce qu'on voit pourrait bien être quelque chose, et pourrait bien aussi n'être rien.... Ils soutiennent avec un sang-froid prodigieux que tout n'était qu'un jeu," and in the *Encyclopédie* article "Pyrrhonienne ou sceptique," A.-T. XVI, 492: "Que dirai-je à celui qui, prétendant que, quoi qu'il voie, quoi qu'il touche, qu'il entende, qu'il aperçoive, ce n'est pourtant jamais que sa sensation qu'il aperçoit...? Je sentirai tout à coup l'absurdité et la profondeur de ce paradoxe; et je me garderai bien de perdre mon temps à détruire dans un homme une opinion qu'il n'a pas, et à qui je n'ai rien à opposer de plus clair que ce qu'il nie."

"sentiment" to express not an effusion of emotion or passion which would help us to judge, but that faculty which judges intuitively, immediately, and which creates judgments which perhaps cannot be justified in rational terms. For example:

That alone, therefore, is to be called a man's opinion, which is of any other the most habitual to him and occurs upon most occasions.... If a man's thoughts are not at all times steady and resolute againt all imagination of chance, fortune, or ill design in things, he is no perfect Theist. *Inquiry,* 241)

Qu'est-ce que *l'opinion* d'un homme? celle qui lui est habituelle. C'est l'hypothèse à laquelle il revient toujours, et non celle dont il n'est jamais sorti, que nous appellerons *son sentiment*.... Si l'on n'est pas constamment éloigné de toute idée de hasard ou de mauvais génie, on n'est pas parfait *théiste.* *C'est le sentiment dominant qui détermine l'état.** (*Essai,* 22; *my italics)

And indeed whatever exterior helps or succors an ill-disposed creature may find to push him on towards the performance of any one good action, there can no goodness arise in him till his temper be so far changed that in the issue he comes in earnest to be led by some immediate affection, directly and not accidentally, to do good and against ill. (*Inquiry,* 249)

En effet, quels que soient les secours étrangers qui vous ont incliné vers le bien, quoi que ce soit qui vous ait prêté main forte contre vos inclinations perverses, tant que vous conserverez le même caractère, je ne verrai point en vous de bonté: vous ne serez bon que quand vous ferez le bien d'affection et de *cœur.* (*Essai,* 34)

"Quand vous ferez le bien ... de cœur," you will be virtuous, in a sense, spontaneously, without consideration of personal gain.

In one instance in the *Essai* "sentiment intérieur" is in fact used to describe man's *instinct* for procreation:

Such concern and care has Nature shown for the support and maintenance of the several species, that by a certain *indigence* and kind of necessity of their natures they are made to regard the propagation of their kind. (*Inquiry,* 324)

Telle est l'attention de la nature à l'entretien de chaque système, que, par une espèce de besoin animal, et par *je ne sais quel sentiment intérieur* d'une indigence qu'elle a placé dans les créatures qui les composent, elle convie les sexes à s'approcher et à s'occuper ensemble de la perpétuité de leur espèce. (*Essai,* 108)

Elsewhere, "cœur" appears to be a synonym of "sentiment intérieur":

In these vagrant characters or pictures of manners, which the mind of necessity figures to itself and carries still about with it, the heart cannot possibly remain neutral; but constantly takes part one way or other. However false or corrupt it be within itself, it finds the difference, as to beauty and comeliness, between one heart and another, one turn of affection, one behaviour, one sentiment and another; and accordingly, in all disinterested cases, must approve in some measure of what is natural and honest, and disapprove what is dishonest and corrupt. (*Inquiry,* 252)	Mais le cœur regarde-t-il avec indifférence les esquisses des mœurs que l'esprit est forcé de tracer, et qui lui sont presque toujours présents? *Je m'en rapporte au sentiment intérieur.* Il me dit qu'aussi nécessité dans ses jugements que l'esprit dans ses opérations, sa corruption ne va jamais jusqu'à lui dérober totalement la différence du beau et du laid, et qu'il ne manquera pas d'approuver le naturel et l'honnête, et de rejeter le déshonnête et le dépravé, surtout dans les moments désintéréressés: *c'est alors un connaisseur équitable qui se promène dans une galerie de peintures, qui s'émerveille de la hardiesse de ce trait, qui sourit à la douceur de ce sentiment, qui se prête au tour de cette affection, et qui passe dédaigneusement sur tout ce qui blesse la belle nature.* (*Essai,* 34-35)

One can see here in the image developed in Diderot's translation just how far he extends the relationship of esthetic and ethical judgments.

"Sense" is generally rendered by Diderot as "sentiment," and accordingly, Shaftesbury's "sense of right and wrong" (*Inquiry,* 258) is translated, to mention only two cases, as "ce sentiment intérieur" and "le sentiment naturel d'injustice et d'équité"

(*Essai*, 41, 42).[27] Although Shaftesbury believes that the moral sense is natural to us — that we are endowed, at birth, with certain judging faculties — Diderot makes this point more explicit than Shaftesbury allows it to appear in the *Inquiry*.

That which is of original and pure nature, nothing beside contrary habit and custom (a second nature) is able to displace. And this affection being an original one of earliest rise in the soul or affectionate part, nothing beside contrary affection, by frequent check and control, can operate upon it, so as either to diminish it in part or destroy it in part or destroy it in the whole. (*Inquiry*, 260)	Déplacer ce qui nous est naturel, c'est l'ouvrage d'une longue habitude: autre nature. Or, la distinction d'injustice et *d'équité nous est originelle: apercevoir dans les êtres intellectuels et moraux laideur et beauté, c'est une opération aussi naturelle, et peu-être antérieure dans notre esprit à l'opération semblable sur les êtres organisés*. Il n'y a donc qu'un exercice contraire qui puisse la troubler pour toujours ou la suspendre pour un temps. (*Essai*, 44)

Conscience itself is a "sentiment intérieur":

There are two things which to a rational creature must be horridly offensive and grievous, viz. 'To have the reflection in his mind of any unjust action or behaviour which he knows to be naturally odious and ill-deserving; or of any foolish action or behaviour which he knows to be prejudicial to his own interest or happiness.' The former of these is alone properly called Conscience, whether as a moral or religious sense. (*Inquiry*, 305)	Deux choses qui doivent horriblement tourmenter toute créature raisonnable, c'est le *sentiment intérieur* d'une action injuste ou d'une conduite odieuse à ses semblables, ou le souvenir d'une action extravagante, ou d'une conduite prejudiciable à ses intérêts et à son bonheur. De ces tourments, c'est le premier qu'on appelle proprement, en morale ou théologie, conscience. (*Essai*, 89)

And in at least one case, "cœur" translates "conscience":

---

[27] See, in Shaftesbury, "a plain internal sensation" (*Moralists*, 63); "an inward eye" (*Moralists*, 137).

And this is a reproach which a mind must of necessity make to itself upon the least violation of natural conscience, in doing what is morally deformed and ill-deserving, though warranted by any example or precedent amongst men, or by any supposed injunction or command of higher powers. (*Inquiry*, 308)

Voila ce qu'un moment de réflexion ne manquera pas d'apprendre à quiconque, entraîné par l'exemple de ses semblables, ou bien effrayé par des ordres supérieurs, sera tenté de prêter sa main à des actions que son cœur désapprouvera. (*Essai*, 93)

4. *Virtue and the Passions.*

A. Textual Modifications.

Diderot apparently makes no distinction in translating Shaftesbury's "passion," "affection," "inclination," and he uses several terms indiscriminately to no clear purpose. In order to present only some examples of this, I point out that on page 72 of the *Essai*, in the space of a single paragraph, Diderot translates "natural affections" (or "natural affection") variously as "passions sociales," "inclinations sociales," and "affection sociale" (see *Inquiry*, 288). Twice on page 73 "passions" is translated as "affections" (*Inquiry*, 289) or, in one instance, "passion" becomes "penchant," but on page 79, "affections" is rendered simply by "affections." Our effort to distinguish between these terms is confounded further by Diderot's enumeration on page 75: "Il serait curieux de parcourir les différents tons des passions, les modes divers des affections, et toutes ces mesures de sentiments qui différencient les caractères entre eux" (see *Inquiry*, 291, where Shaftesbury more succinctly suggests that "It might be agreable, one would think, to inquire thus into the different tunings of the passions, the various mixtures and allays by which men become so different from one another"). Still, all of these words designate in the *Essai* feeling or emotion, the instinctual or irrational constituent of the psyche, and, as we have said, one must conclude that Diderot thinks of these terms — "passion," "penchant," "inclination," "sentiment," "affection" — as fundamentally synonymous and therefore interchangeable for his purposes as translator.

Both Diderot and Shaftesbury believe that virtue consists in part of a mastery of that irrational side of the psyche which is vaguely termed the "passions." A noteworthy addition to this effect is inserted into the text of page 70 of the *Essai*:

The latter sort of these affections [those which are conducive neither to public good or private good], 'tis evident, are wholly vicious. The two former affections which lead to public good *or* private good may be vicious or virtuous according to their degree.(*Inquiry*, 286)	Il est évident que la dernière espèce d'affections est toute vicieuse. Quant aux deux autres, elles peuvent être bonnes ou mauvaises, selon leur degré. *Elles maîtrisent toujours la créature purement sensible; mais la créature sensible et raisonnable peut toujours les maîtriser, quelques puissantes qu'elles soient.* (*Essai*, 70)

Such an addition should adequately demonstrate how far Diderot is in 1745 from advocating a liberation of the passions from the constraint of reason: the key concept here is one of *balance* between the *sensible* and the *raisonnable*.

B. The *Discours préliminaire* and Footnote Additions.

That virtue entails the control of the passions is stated in the *Discours préliminaire*: "L'homme est intègre ou vertueux, lorsque, sans aucun motif bas et servile, tel que l'espoir d'une récompense ou la crainte d'un châtiment, il contraint toutes ses passions à conspirer au bien général de son espèce: effort héroïque, et qui toutefois n'est jamais contraire à ses intérêts particuliers" (*Essai*, 13). Likewise, in note 1, page 30, Diderot sketches a hierarchy of goodness, the highest form of which is "Une bonté raisonnée, propre à l'être pensant, qu'on appelle Vertu: qualité qui est d'autant plus méritoire en lui, qu'étaient grandes les mauvaises dispositions qui constituent la méchanceté animale, et qu'il avait à vaincre pour parvenir à la bonté raisonnée." Virtue is superior to a kind of natural goodness, a "bonté animale," which consists only of "une économie dans les passions, que toute créature sensible et bien constituée reçoit de la nature. C'est en ce sens, qu'on dit d'un chien de chasse, lorsqu'il est bon, qu'il n'est ni lâche, ni opiniâtre, ni lent, ni emporté, ni timide, ni indocile, mais ardent, intelligent et prompt." [28] Lucidity is indispensable to virtuous conduct; one who does good by accident, because he is endowed naturally with a temperament disposed to goodness, is not worthy of being called virtuous. "Nous naissons tous plus ou moins dépravés; les uns timides, ambitieux et colères; les autres avares, indolents et téméraires; mais cette dépravation involontaire du tempérament ne rend point, par elle-même, la créature vicieuse: au contraire, elle sert à relever son mérite lorsqu'elle en triomphe": since we are all naturally less than perfectly good — since we are all possessed of a certain *"méchanceté* animale" — the achievement of virtue requires a conscious effort at self-control. Virtue is largely a matter of willing. [29]

But if the passions must be controlled, they should not be stifled; a certain balance or economy is to be achieved in one's affective life: "Nous ressemblons à de vrais instruments dont les passions sont les cordes. Dans le fou, elles sont trop hautes; l'instrument crie: elles sont trop basses dans le stupide; l'instrument est sourd. Un homme sans passions est donc un instrument dont on a coupé les cordes, ou qui n'en eut jamais" (*Essai*, note 1, 75). This famous image of man as a musical instrument will of course be used several times later in Diderot's career, but it seems that its source is to be found in Shaftesbury's *Inquiry*:

> Upon the whole, it may be said properly to be the same with the affections or passions in an animal constitution as with the cords or strings of a musical instrument. If these, though in ever so just proportion one to another, are strained beyond a certain degree, 'tis more than the

---

[28] It would appear that Diderot's definitions of *bonté animale* and *vertu* are inspired by Shaftesbury's statement at the beginning of Part II, section III: "But to proceed from what is esteemed mere goodness, and lies within the reach and capacity of all sensible creatures, to that which is called virtue or merit, and is allowed to man only" (*Inquiry*, 251). Which sentence Diderot translates thus: "Mais pour passer de cette bonté pure et simple, dont toute créature sensible est capable, à cette qualité qu'on appelle vertu, et qui convient ici-bas à l'homme seul" (*Essai*, 32)[.] A.-T. wrongly ends the sentence with a question mark.

[29] It is difficult therefore to agree with Jacques Roger's recent assessment of "nature" in the *Essai:* "Diderot se sent naturellement bon, bon par un élan immédiat du cœur, dans lequel la raison, cette 'rivale' des passions, n'a rien à voir" ("Le Déisme du jeune Diderot," in *Europäische Aufklärung*, p. 291).

instrument will bear: the lute or lyre is abused, and its effect lost. On the other hand, if while some of the strings are duly strained, others are not wound up to their due proportion, then is the instrument still in disorder, and its part ill performed. (*Inquiry*, 290)

Diderot apparently thought the image so apt that his modifications of a passage some paragraphs *earlier* suggest the musical comparison.

| But if to have all the passions in equal proportion with it, be what the constitution of the creature cannot bear, so that only some passions are raised to this height, whilst others are not, nor can possibly be wrought up to the same proportion, then may those strong passions, though of the better wind, be called excessive. (*Inquiry*, 289) | Mais si la constitution naturelle de la créature ne permet pas au reste des affections de monter à son *unisson*, si le *ton* des unes est aussi haut, et celui des autres plus bas, quelle que soit la nature des unes et des autres, elles pécheront par excès ou par défaut.... (*Essai*, 73) |

Diderot begins note 1, page 75 by commenting on the point made in the text; "Nous ressemblons à de vrais instruments ... l'instrument est sourd." Then in fact he already begins to extend Shaftesbury's analogy, and he suggests that "un homme sans passions est donc un instrument dont on a coupé les cordes, ou qui n'en eut jamais." At this point Diderot indicates that he is adding ideas of his own to the metaphor suggested by Shaftesbury ("C'est ce qu'on a déjà dit"): "Mais il y a plus. Si quand un instrument est d'accord, vous en pincez une corde, le son qu'elle rend occasionne des frémissements, et dans les instruments voisins, si leurs cordes ont une tension proportionellement harmonique avec la corde pincée; et dans ses voisines, sur le même instrument, si elles gardent avec elle la même proportion." This sentence contrasts with what we are told in the text of page 75: there Shaftesbury emphasizes the *diversity* of the "different sorts of instruments," with respect to the various systems of beings and within each system itself. Diderot however speculates upon the internal harmony of a single instrument *and* upon possibility or harmony among numerous instruments — the possibility, that is, of a concert. He thus expands what in Shaftesbury remains for the most part a metaphor for internal affective harmony into an image of a kind of emotional harmony among the components of society as well: "Image parfaite de l'affinité des rapports et de la conspiration mutuelle de certaines affections dans le même caractère, et des impressions gracieuses et du doux frémissement que les belles actions excitent dans les autres, surtout lorsqu'ils sont vertueux." The comparison of man to a musical instrument finally develops then into the image of *moral* harmony in the "concert de la société" (*Essai*, 75): "belles actions" are echoed by similar deeds — "Cette comparaison pourrait être poussée bien loin, car le son excité est toujours analogue à celui qui l'excite."

5. *Virtue and Self-Interest.*

A. Textual Modifications.

Several modifications and additions in the *Essai* demonstrate that Diderot judged Shaftesbury's treatment of self-interest in the *Inquiry* to be inadequate, and he generally presents self-interest in a better light than Shaftesbury gives it in the original text.

We know that every creature has a private good and interest of his own, which Nature has compelled him to seek, by all the advantages afforded him within the compass of his make. (*Inquiry*, 243)	Cependant nous savons que chaque créature a un *intérêt privé*, un *bien-être* qui lui est propre, et auquel elle tend de toute sa puissance; *penchant raisonnable* * qui a son origine dans les avantages de sa conformation naturelle. (*Essai*, 23; *my italics)

In another case Diderot underlines the intrinsic goodness of self-interest:

But if the affection be then only injurious to the society when it is immoderate, and not so when it is moderate, duly tempered, and allayed, then is the immoderate degree of the affection truly vicious, but not	Mais si le penchant à ses intérêts privés n'est injurieux à la société que quand il est excessif, et jamais lorsqu'il est tempéré, nous dirons alors que l'excès a rendu vicieux un penchant qui *dans sa nature était*

the moderate. And thus if there be found in any creature a more than ordinary self-concernment or regard to private good, which is inconsistent with the interest of the species or public, this must in every respect be esteemed an ill and vicious affection. And this is what we commonly call selfishness, and disapprove so much in whatever creature we happen to discover it. (*Inquiry*, 248)	*bon.* Ainsi toute inclination qui portera la créature à son bien particulier, *pour être vicieuse, doit être nuisible à l'intérêt public.* C'est ce défaut qui caractérise l'homme intéressé, défaut contre lequel on se récrie si haut, *quand il est trop marqué.* (*Essai*, 29)

While Shaftesbury is intent upon condemning excessive self-interest in the above passage, Diderot, in his translation, repeatedly returns to the *defense* of a human drive which he finds to be basically good.[30]

Similarly, on page 49 of the Essai, where it is a question of those passions which oppose our sense of right and wrong, and even our own well-being, Diderot replaces "self-interest" with "bonheur" (see *Inquiry*, 265). Later, where Shaftesbury distinguishes the "natural affections" and the "self affections" (see *Inquiry*, 286), Diderot efface the opposition and refers to both kinds as "des affections naturelles" (*Essai*, 70), apparently believing that Shaftesbury's terms made self-interest appear unnatural, and therefore inferior in value to those affections "which lead to the good of the public." Once again finally, in Book II, Part II, section II, Diderot notes that it is in the "degré d'*intensité*" that the "self-passions" are harmful to the individual and to society (*Essai*, 102; Diderot's emphasis; compare *Inquiry*, 317).

B. Footnote Additions.

Note 1, page 29 is adapted from *An Essay on the Freedom of Wit and Humour* (ed. Robertson, I, 120-21), and it serves to

---

[30] Roger asserts that the "affirmation de la bonté de l'homme est le thème majeur de l'*Essai sur le mérite et la vertu*," and rightly points out that "l'intérêt lui-même, comme toute forme de l'amour de soi, est légitime en son principe et ne devient coupable que par excès" ("Le Déisme...," *loc. cit.*, p. 240).

expand the notion of self-interest which is already apparent in the additions at the top of page 29: "Tous les livres de morale sont pleins de déclamations vagues contre l'intérêt." Diderot surely alludes to La Rochefoucauld when he claims that "On s'epuise en détails, en divisions et subdivisions pour en venir à cette conclusion énigmatique, *que, quel que soit le désintéressement spécieux, quelle que soit la générosité apparente dont nous nous parions au fond, l'intérêt el l'amour-propre sont les seuls principes de nos actions*" (Diderot's italics). The description of the fundamental social and moral *illusion* and the formula of the concession which is almost immediately withdrawn — "*quel que soit ... l'intérêt et l'amour-propre sont les seuls principes....*" — these are techniques familiar to any reader of the *Maximes*. And in fact, Diderot accuses La Rochefoucauld, and writers like him, of bad faith, of being more concerned with style and *esprit* than with conceptual precision: "Si au lieu de courir après l'esprit, et d'arranger des phrases, ces auteurs, partant de définitions exactes, avaient commencé par nous apprendre ce que c'est qu'intérêt, ce qu'ils entendent par amour-propre, leurs ouvrages, avec cette clef, pourraient servir à quelque chose." Diderot, unlike La Rochefoucauld, does not see an antipathy of self-interest and virtue: "Car nous sommes tous d'accord que la créature peut s'aimer, peut tendre à ses intérêts, et poursuivre son bonheur temporel, sans cesser d'être vertueuse." We can therefore dispense with subtle psychological distinctions, for the important thing in the last analysis is to know, not, after the fact, *if* we have acted according to *amour-propre* or *intérêt*, but more pragmatically, when, and to what extent, and how, self-interest is conducive to the highest good — happiness. Self-interest, virtue, and happiness, are not, Diderot says in this instance, antagonistic; happiness in fact involves a clear *understanding* of the value of one's own desires: "Le dernier effort de la prudence humaine, c'est de s'aimer, c'est d'entendre ses intérêts, c'est de connaître son bonheur comme il faut."

Diderot's conclusion does not in the last analysis, differ essentially from that of Shaftesbury:

> For in this we should all agree, that happiness was to be pursued, and in fact was always sought after: but whether

> found in following Nature, and giving way to common affection; or in suppressing it, and turning every passion towards private advantage, a narrow self-end, or the preservation of more life; this would be the matter in debate between us. The question would not be, 'who loved himself, or who not;' but "who loved served himself the rightest, and after the truest manner.' (*Freedom*, 121) [31]

Virtue is simply the best means of achieving one's happiness. If, as we have seen, Diderot at times thinks of virtue as an effort and a sacrifice, it seems that he is attempting to retain the concept of virtue as a balancing of self-interest and altruism. In theory at least; for, as we have also already noticed, whether virtuous behavior actually brings us bliss on this earth is another matter for Diderot.

Relative to this question of happiness, self-interest, and virtue, one should cite note 1, page 65:

> .... Nous sommes chacun, dans la société, ce qu'est une partie, relativement à un tout organisé. La mesure du temps est la propriété essentielle d'une montre; *le bonheur des particuliers est la fin principale de la société.* Ces effets, ou ne se produiront point, ou ne se proudiront qu'aimparfaitement, sans une conspiration mutuelle des parties dans la montre et des membres dans la société. Si quelque roue se dérange, la mesure du temps sera suspendue ou troublée; si quelque particulier occupe une place qui n'étaient point faite pour lui, le bien général en souffrira, ou même s'anéantira; et la société ne sera plus que l'image d'une montre détraquée.

Roger Lewinter's interpretation of this passage,

> La société... est comme un grand corps à l'intérieur duquel les hommes ne sont que de simples organes dont la fin est de contribuer au bon fonctionnement de l'ensemble. Désormais est bon ce qui est socialement bon, *et non plus ce qui l'est individuellement;* l'utilité pratique l'importe sur la vérité pure. Morale de l'utilité, la morale

---

[31] We note again that Shaftesbury's remarks are directed against Hobbes, and again Diderot ignores the allusion to Hobbes.

> de l'*Essai* repose sur l'exaltation de l'ordre établi et du devoir, et le premier devoir de l'individu est de rester dans cadres de sa condition. [32]

seems to me to be a misreading. Diderot very clearly says that "le bonheur des particuliers est la fin principale de la société," and as we have seen, he is very careful in his modifications of the text of the *Essai* to see that our drives of self-interest are not scorned. As the clock image suggests, if the mechanism of society is perfectly and delicated balanced, society *and* the individual will benefit.

---

[32] In "L'Exaltation de la vertu dans le théâtre de Diderot," *Diderot Studies VIII*, Geneva, Droz, 1966, p. 125.

CHAPTER II

THE STYLE OF THE *ESSAI*

I. The *Discours préliminaire* and Textual Modifications.

In the *Discours préliminaire* of the *Essai* Diderot justifies his offering a translation of Shaftesbury's *Inquiry* by asserting that such a text fulfills a need in France for a *practical* ethical guide. We are told that French moralists and philosophers have failed to provide us with fundamental ethical insight and guidance — on the one hand, because they have been too much concerned with metaphysics and theory, and on the other, because they have but generalized about human conduct instead of suggesting valid means of correcting those failings which they only too carefully point out.[1] These reproaches are aimed specifically at the representatives of the scholastic tradition and the writers of "maximes."[2]

---

[1] We recall the objections of Descartes to the ineffectual ethical teachings of the Ancients: "Je comparais les écrits des anciens païens, qui traitent des mœurs, à des palais fort superbes et fort magnifiques, qui n'étaient bâtis que sur du sable et sur de la boue. Ils élèvent fort haut les vertus, et les font paraître estimables par-dessus toutes les choses qui sont au monde; mais ils n'enseignent pas assez à les connaître, et souvent ce qu'ils appellent d'un si beau nom, n'est qu'une insensibilité, ou un orgueil, ou un désespoir, ou un parricide" (*Discours de la Méthode, première partie*).

[2] Diderot cites only La Bruyère, but he would certainly place La Rochefoucauld and Pascal in this category as well. For an allusion to La Rochefoucauld, see note 1, page 29 of the *Essai* and our Chapter I. It is interesting to compare Diderot's opinion to the comments of the author of "Le Philosophe": "Le philosophe forme ses principes sur une infinité d'observations particulières; le peuple adopte le principe sans penser aux observations qui l'ont produit: il croit que la maxime existe, pour ainsi dire,

> Nous ne manquons pas de longs traités de morale; mais on n'a point encore pensé à nous en donner des *éléments;* car je ne peux appeler de ce nom ni ces conclusions futiles qu'on nous dicte à la hâte dans les écoles, et qu'heureusement on n'a pas le temps d'expliquer, ni ces recueils de maximes sans liaison et sans ordre, où l'on a pris à tâche de déprimer l'homme, sans s'occuper beaucoup de le corriger. Ce n'est pas qu'il n'y ait quelque différence à faire entre ces deux sortes d'ouvrages: j'avoue qu'il y a plus à profiter dans une page de La Bruyère que dans le volume entier de Pourchot; mais il faut convenir aussi qu'ils sont les uns et les autres incapables de rendre un lecteur vertueux *par principes.*
> (*Essai,* 11)

What we need then are cogently presented "éléments," "principes": practical, useful rules of *morale*. As it is, philosophy is no longer borne out in action — it no longer influences our lives; students are taught Cartesian subtleties and a knowledge of nature instead of practical ethical values and a knowledge of man:

> Un jeune homme, au sortir de son cours de philosophie, est jeté dans un monde d'athées, de déistes, de sociniens, de spinosistes et d'autres impies; fort instruit des propriétés de la matière subtile et de la formation des tourbillons, connaissances merveilleuses qui lui devienent parfaitement inutiles; mais à peine sait-il des avantages de la vertu ce que lui en dit un précepteur, ou des fondements de sa religion ce qu'il en a lu dans son catéchisme.
> (*Essai,* 12) [3]

Diderot points out therefore that the goal of Shaftesbury's *Inquiry* is to show that a sound practical knowledge of ethics and

---

par elle-même; mais le philosophe prend la maxime dès sa source; il en examine l'origine, il en connaît la propre valeur, et n'en fait que l'usage qui lui convient" (cited in Herbert Dieckmann, *"Le Philosophe": Texts and Interpretation,* St. Louis, 1948, p. 32).

[3] Compare *Pensées philosophiques* XX: "C'était en vain que j'avais essayé contre un athée les subtilités de l'école; il avait même tiré de la faiblesse de ces raisonnements une objection assez forte. 'Une multitude de vérités inutiles me sont démontrées sans réplique, disait-il; et l'existence de Dieu, la réalité du bien et du mal moral, l'immortalité de l'âme, sont encore des problèmes pour moi. Quoi doncl me serait-il moins important d'être éclairé sur ces sujets, que d'être convaincu que les trois angles d'un triangle sont égaux à deux droits?' "

conduct is indispensable to all of us: "Le but de cet ouvrage est de montrer que la vertu est presque indivisiblement attachée à la connaissance de Dieu, et que le bonheur temporel de l'homme est inséparable de la vertu" (*Essai*, 12). Moreover, Diderot maintains that he has improved upon the English original — and primarily by adding his own "réflexions":

> J'ai resserré ce qui m'a paru trop diffus, étendu ce qui m'a paru trop serré, rectifié ce qui n'était pensé qu'avec hardiesse; et les réflexions qui accompagnent cette espèce de texte sont si fréquentes, que l'*Essai* de M.... S.... qui n'etait proprement qu'une *démonstration métaphysique*, s'est converti en éléments de *morales* assez considérables. (*Essai*, 16)

Diderot claims that he has thus transformed a work of theory into a work of *practical* value — here at last is an *elementary* treatise, something which will *show* us how virtue and happiness are achieved (and indeed, Diderot's translation was in fact published in Amsterdam — Paris — with the title *Principes de la philosophie morale; ou Essai de M.S.*** sur le mérite et la vertu*). An examination of the *Essai* and the English original shows that Diderot has attempted to effect his presentation of "éléments de morale" by providing *examples* — drawn from what is presented as his own experience, from history or literature or philosophy, or from his own imagination. Diderot tries to bring Shaftesbury's *Inquiry* down to earth, to demonstrate how the argument is applied to *life*. It is in this basic sense that Diderot's translation of the *Inquiry* is "personal," more vivid, more concrete, than the original, because Diderot involves himself and his reader in the argument. Diderot often intrudes, both in his interpolations within the text and in the notes, in order to establish an intimate rapport with his reader. One of the most obvious stylistic alterations made of the original text by Diderot is the very frequent substitution of "je" where Shaftesbury, in the anonymity of elevated style,[4] uses "we" or an even more neutral expression —

---

[4] Bonamy Dobrée's assessment of Shaftesbury's style might be recalled here: "His style, a little too urbane saving where he waxes rhapsodical, somewhat muffles his attack" (*English Literature in the Early Eighteenth Century*, Oxford, 1959, p. 262).

as, for example, in the very first paragraph of the *Essai:* "It may however be questioned whether the practice of the world in this respect be answerable to our speculation" (*Inquiry*, 237); "*Je* doute cependant que cette idée scrupuleuse soit confirmée par la connaissance du monde...." (*Essai*, 17). Or again in Book I, Part I, Section I:

When we reflect on any ordinary frame or constitution either of Art or Nature, and consider how hard it is to give the least account of a particular part without a competent knowledge of the whole.... (*Inquiry*, 243)	Lorsque *je* tourne les yeux sur les ouvrages d'un artiste, ou sur quelque production ordinaire de la nature, et que *je sens en moi-même* combien il est difficile de parler avec exactitude des parties, sans une connaissance profonde du tout.... (*Essai*, 23)

Diderot, already in this his first work of any originality, shows deep concern with the presence of his reader, who in many cases becomes an imagined interlocutor or adversary. "Quiconque n'a pas la force ou le courage de suivre un raisonnement étendu, peut se dispenser de commencer la lecture de cet ouvrage; c'est pour d'autres que j'ai travaillé," he warns in the *Discours préliminaire*. [5] The end of the first paragraph of the *Essai* offers an example of what will become Diderot's characteristic practice of seeing himself involved in dialogue:

And in general, we find mere moral principles [6] of such weight, than in our dealings	En général, on a beau nous assurer qu'un homme est plein de zèle pour sa religion, si nous

---

[5] See Herbert Dieckmann, *Cinq leçons sur Diderot*, Geneva and Paris, 1959, p. 24, where it is noted, with regard to the dedication of the *Essai* to the brother of Diderot, that "Diderot ne fait pas de doute que le problème des rapports entre la morale et la religion se pose pour lui non seulement dans les termes d'une situation historique ou d'une position philosophique déterminée par Shaftesbury, Spinoza, Bayle et Descartes, mais aussi dans la perspective d'un conflit profond et d'un dialogue avec son frere, dialogue qui devait durer longtemps. L' *Essai* est adressé à une personne concrète, le frère de Diderot."

[6] Diderot generally renders "principles" and "rules" by "principes"; see, for example, *Essai*, 18 (*Inquiry*, 237-38) and *Essai*, 17 (*Inquiry*, 237). In the *Essai* itself, the example of a slight alteration of the English text reveals

with men we are seldom satisfied by the fullest assurance given us of their zeal in religion, till we hear something further of their character. If we are told a man is religious, we still ask, "What are his morals?" But if we hear at first that he has honest moral principles, and is a man of natural justice and good temper, we seldom think of the other question, "Whether he be religious and devout?" (*Inquiry*, 237-38)	avons à traiter avec lui, nous nous informons encore de son caractère. "*M*** a de la religion*, dites-vous; mais *a-t-il de la probité?*" Si vous m'eussiez fait entendre d'abord qu'il était honnête homme, je ne me serais jamais avisé de demander s'il était *dévot*: TANT EST GRANDE SUR NOS ESPRITS L'AUTORITÉ DES PRINCIPES MORAUX. (*Essai*, 17-18)

Although Shaftesbury conceives his posing the question "What are his morals?" Diderot, by positing a "vous," renders the confrontation a *present* (Shaftesbury: "If we hear....") personal exchange with an "opponent."

If Diderot substitutes "je" for "we," he as often will replace Shaftesbury's "one," "he," or "him," or an impersonal passive voice construction with "vous" and direct address:

In the first place, then, it may be observed that if there be an affection towards any subject considered as private good.... (*Essai*, 247)	*Remarquez* d'abord que toute affection, qui a pour objet un bien imaginaire.... (*Essai*, 28)

---

further that Diderot associates a knowledge of "principes" and an active — not theoretical — application of moral rules.

So that if a creature be generous, kind, constant, compassionate, yet if he cannot reflect on what he himself does, or sees others do, so as to take notice of what is worthy or honest, and make that notice or conception of worth and honesty to be an object of his affection, he has not the character of being virtuous; for thus, and no otherwise, he is capable of having a sense of right and wrong, a sentiment of judgment of what is done through just, equal, and good affection, or the contrary. (*Inquiry*, 253)	Qu'une créature soit généreuse, douce, affable, ferme et compatissante; si jamais elle n'a réfléchi sur ce qu'elle pratique et voit pratiquer aux autres; si elle ne s'est fait aucune idée *nette* et *précise* du bien et du mal; si les charmes de la vertu et de l'honnêteté ne sont point les objets de son affection; son caractère n'est point vertueux *par principes;* elle en est encore à acquérir *cette connaissance active de la droiture* qui devait la déterminer, cet amour désintéressé de la vertu qui seul pouvait donner tout le prix à ses actions. (*Essai*, 36)

.... Let him, in any particular, act ever so well, if at bottom it be that selfish affection alone which moves him, he is in himself still vicious. (*Inquiry*, 249)

.... *Illustrez-vous* par de grandes actions tant qu'il *vous* plaira, *vous* serez vicieux tant que *vous* n'agirez que par des principes intéressés. (*Essai*, 30)

Where Shaftesbury says "A person, for instance, who has much of goodness and natural rectitude in his temper...." (*Inquiry*, 270-71), Diderot renders "Imaginez un homme qui ait quelque bonté naturelle...." (*Essai*, 54), and the encouragement to *visualize* is to be taken literally. The theoretical becomes real, it is to be seen — or to be *touched:*

It has been already shown, that in the passions and affections of particular creatures there is a constant relation to the interest of a species or common nature. (*Inquiry*, 280)

Nous avons démontré que les affections d'une créature quelconque avaient un rapport constant et déterminé avec l'intérêt général de son espèce. *C'est une vérité que nous avons fait toucher au doigt*.... (*Essai*, 64)

Diderot's textual modifications and additions to the *Inquiry* demonstrate that he already senses the heuristic potential of dialogue and debate: in the following case, while Shaftesbury only suggests the possibility of an objection to his point, Diderot imagines the *réplique* as it would be made by his "opponent," and he furnishes the response.

.... As when pity is so overcome as to destroy its own end, and prevent the succour and relief required; or as when love to the offspring proves such a fondness as destroys the parent, and consequently the offspring itself. And notwithstanding it may seem harsh to call that unnatural and vicious which is only an extreme of some natural and kind affection, yet 'tis most certain that wherever any single good affection of this sort is over-great, it must be injurious to the rest, and detract in some

Lors, par exemple, que la commisération est si vive qu'elle manque son but, en suprimant par son excès les secours qu'on a droit d'en attendre; lorsque la tendresse maternelle est si violente qu'elle perd la mère, et par conséquent, l'enfant avec elle. "Mais, dira-t-on, traiter de vicieux et de dénaturé ce qui n'est que l'excès de quelque affection naturelle et généreuse, n'y aurait-il pas en cela un rigorisme mal entendu?" Pour toute réponse à cette objection, je remarquerai, que la meilleure

measure from their force and natural operation. *Inquiry,* 286)

affection dans sa nature suffit, par son intensité, pour endommager toutes ses compagnes, pour restreindre leur énergie et ralentir ou suspendre leurs opérations. (*Essai,* 70-71)

Examples of instances in which Diderot transforms Shaftesbury's declarative sentences into *périodes* or rhetorical questions are extraordinarily numerous,[7] a fact which constitutes further evidence that Diderot is inclined to envision himself locked, not simply in written controversy, but in oral debate, which forces him to draw upon his knowledge of the art of persuasion.

Diderot's tendency to think of philosophical controversy in terms of debate leads him, upon occasion, to allow his "personnages" to speak, indirectly, for themselves:

As to interest, how far it is here concerned; how wretched that state in which by this habit a man is placed towards all the circumstances and affairs of life when at any time he is called to action; how subjected he must be to all inconveniencies, wanting to himself, and deprived of the assistance of others; whilst being unfit for all offices and duties of society he as yet of any other person most needs the help of it, as being least able to assist or support himself; all this is obvious. And thus 'tis evident "that to have this overbiassing inclination towards rest, this slothful, soft, or effeminate temper, averse to labour and employment, is to have an unavoidable mis-

Quant à l'intérêt particulier de la créature, il est évident que ce cours effréné de désirs augmentera sa dépendance en multipliant ses besoins; qu'elle ne tardera pas à trouver ses fonds, quelque considérables qu'ils soient, insuffisants pour les dépenses qu'ils exigeront; que, pour satisfaire à cette impérieuse somptuosité, il en faudra aux expédients, sacrifier peut-être son honneur à l'accroissement de ses revenus, et s'abaisser à mille infâmes manoeuvres, pour augmenter sa fortune. *Mais à quoi bon m'occuper à démontrer le tort que le voluptueux se fait à lui-même? laissons-le s'expliquer là-dessus. Dans l'impossibilité de résister au torrent qui l'entraîne, il déclarera en*

---

[7] A complete listing of examples of this change is unnecessary, but see, for instance, *Essai,* 17 (*Inquiry,* 237); *Essai,* 23 (*Inquiry,* 243); *Essai,* 24 (*Inquiry,* 244).

chief and attendant plague." (*Inquiry*, 329)	*s'y abandonant, qu'il s'aperçoit bien qu'il court à une ruine certaine. On a tous les jours l'occasion d'entendre ces discours: j'en ai donc assez dit pour conclure que la volupté, la débauche et tout excès sont contraires aux vrais intérêts et au bonheur présent de la créature.* (*Essai*, 107)

Since we are all acquainted, suggests Diderot, with people who are at odds with the demands of their appetites ("On a tous les jours l'occasion d'entendre ces discours"), if we could but *listen* to the complaints of the *débauché*, we would be more easily convinced of the horrors of incontinence. Diderot inspires the reader to adduce his *own* examples and thus to see the relevance of the general point to the *hic et nunc*. Diderot clearly establishes himself in a personal relationship to the study of virtue and merit, and he is greatly intent upon obliging the reader to do likewise. The reader is encouraged to recognize that philosophy is relevant to real situations and that it can be *used*.

Diderot's tendency to *visualize* and his wish to place his reader in concrete situations — to make him *see* — are further represented by his frequent interpolation of figurative language:

For though he may intend to be virtuous, he is not become so for having only intended or aimed at it through love of the reward. But as soon as he is come to have any affection towards what is morally good for its own sake, as good and amiable in itself, then is he in some degree good and virtuous, and not till then. (*Inquiry*, 273-74)	*Cette créature est tout au plus dans les* avenues, *sur la* route; *après s'être* embarqué *par pur intérêt, la bassesse avouée du motif ne la met point au* port: *en un mot, elle ne sera vertueuse que quant ses efforts feront germer en elle quelque affection pour la bonté morale considérée comme telle, et sans égard à ses intérêts.* (*Essai*, 57)

He who does good only in his own interest is but a *seeker* after virtue, and unless he should come to see that moral good possesses intrinsic value, he will remain lost and never reach home.

At times, the image is only suggested by Shaftesbury, and Diderot makes it explicit, elaborates it, and carries it through with greater consistency.

> He... who is withheld by force or accident, finds in his temper the ill effects of this restraint. The inclination, when suppressed, breeds discontent, and on the contrary affords a healing and enlivening joy when acting at its liberty and with full scope; as we may see particularly when after a time of solitude and long absence the heart is opened, the mind disburdened, and the secrets of the breast unfolded to a bosom friend. (*Inquiry*, 315-16)

> L'homme séquestré, ou celui qui est séparé des hommes et de la société, par accident ou par force, doit éprouver dans son tempérament de funestes effets de cette séparation. La tristesse et la mauvaise humeur s'engendrent partout où l'affection sociale est éteinte ou réprimée; mais a-t-elle occasion d'agir en pleine liberté et de se manifester dans toute son énergie, elle transporte la créature. *Celui dont on a brisé les liens, qui renaît à la lumière au sortir d'un cachot où il a été longtemps détenu, n'est pas plus heureux dans les premiers moments de sa liberté....* (*Essai*, 99-100)

In another instance, Diderot departs even more noticeably from Shaftesbury's narrative and imagines a vivid *scene:*

> A man who in a passion happens to kill his companion, relents immediately on the sight of what he has done. His revenge is changed into pity, and his hatred turned against himself. And this merely by the power of the object. On this account he suffers agonies: the subject of this continually occurs to him, and of this he has a constant ill remembrance and displeasing consciousness. (*Inquiry*, 306-07)

> Un homme qui, dans un premier mouvement, a le malheur de tuer son semblable, revient subitement à la vue de ce qu'il a fait; sa haine se change en pitié, et sa fureur se tourne contre lui-même: tel est le pouvoir de l'objet. *Mais il n'est pas au bout de ses peines; il ne retrouve pas sa tranquillité en perdant de vue le cadavre; il entre ensuite en agonie; le sang du mort coule derechef à ses yeux; il est transi d'horreur, et le sou-*

> *venir cruel de son action le poursuit en tout lieu. (Essai, 91)* [8]

Diderot's short phrases convey the anxiety of the murderer, and the vision of the crime is seen through the eyes of the criminal. The killer is haunted, not by "the object," nor by "the subject of this," but by the *sight* of "le *cadavre*," by the real *presence* of the corpse. Shaftesbury's "of this" becomes then specified as the vision of the deranged assassin: "le sang du mort coule derechef à ses yeux." The limp "constant ill remembrance and displeasing consciousness" is transformed by the vision of Diderot's killer, who becomes a tragic figure, driven, like Racine's Oreste, in perpetual flight from the horrors recreated in his own mind.

II. Footnote Additions

In the note at the bottom of the first page of the *Discours préliminaire*, Diderot adds weight to his contention that scholastic philosophy is antithetical to a knowledge of the world by citing, in English, a passage from *The Moralists*:

> We have immured philosophy (poor Lady!) in colleges and cells.... The *schoolsyllogism* and the *Elixir*, are the choicest of her products. So far is she from producing statesmen as of old, that hardly any man of note in the public cares to own the least obligation to her. If some few maintain their acquaintance, and come now and then to her recesses, it is as the disciple of quality *came* to his lord and master; "*secretly* and *by night.*" Peinture admirable du triste état de la philosophie parmi nous, mais qu'on ne peut rendre dans notre langue avec toute sa force. (*Essai*, 11)

As in this case, Diderot time and time again in his notes has recourse to a dialogue situation in order to extend or modify Shafterbury's argument or to present ideas of his own. In the second of the notes appended to the end of the first paragraph of

---

[8] See also the "architecture morale" image, *Essai*, 98 (*Inquiry*, 314).

the *Essai* proper (p. 18), Diderot delivers, in an aside, advice to his reader:

> Remarquez qu'il est question ici de la religion en général. Si le christianisme était un culte universellement embrassé, quand on assurerait d'un homme qu'il est bon chrétien, peut-être serait-il absurde de demander s'il est honnête homme; parce qu'il n'y a point, dirait-on, de christianisme réel sans probité. Mais il y a presque autant de cultes différents que de gouvernements; et si nous en croyons les histoires, leurs préceptes croisent souvent les principes de la morale; ce qui suffit pour justifier ma pensée....

But Diderot is not satisfied with a statement of such general import, and he reinforces his argument by saying to the reader in effect, "This is how the problem reveals itself in a particular situation...."

> Mais, *afin de lui donner toute l'évidence possible, supposé que*, dans un besoin pressant de secours, on vous adressât à quelque juif opulent.... (*Essai*, 18, note 2)

Note 1, pages 26-27, contains another "argument" — this time between "ceux qui attaquent la nature" and Diderot, who represents "ceux qui la défendent," and, as we have noted in Chapter I, in the long note of page 33, Diderot opposes the position taken by Shaftesbury in *The Moralists* that beauty exists only in art and not in the object described.

In note 1, page 33, in which Diderot proclaims the dangerous consequences of preaching atheism, rather than simply *cite* Shaftesbury, he conceives the manner in which Shaftesbury himself would *address* those bent upon persuading us of the validity of their views: "Il me semble que *j'entends* M. S. qui *dit* à un de ces docteurs: 'La philosophie que vous avez la bonté de me révéler est tout à fait extraordinaire....'" [9]

---

[9] The source for Shaftesbury's "words" is *Freedom of Wit and Humour*, in *Characteristics*, I, 63. Moreover, *Freedom*, unlike *The Moralists*, is direct discourse, not dialogue.

Later, in the dialogue with the *Pyrrhonien* (*Essai*, 119, note), Diderot debates the problem of personal identity as it influences action, and then imposes his own conclusion. Elsewhere Diderot forces his *adversaire dévot* to reveal his own doctrinal insecurity:

> .... je demanderais volontiers si les inégalités dans la dévotion peuvent s'accorder avec des notions constantes de la Divinité. Si votre Dieu ne change point, pourquoi n'êtes-vous pas ferme dans la même assiette d'esprit? Je ne sais, dites-vous, s'il me pardonnera les fautes passées, et j'en fais tous les jours de nouvelles. Etes-vous encore méchant, j'approve vos alarmes, et je suis étonné qu'elles ne soient continuelles.... (*Essai*, 90 note)

Near the end of the *Essai*, in order to support Shaftesbury's conclusion that "the greatest of miseries accompanies that state which is consequent to the loss of natural affection," Diderot turns to the records of history for documentation:

> Je ne crois qu'on trouve jamais l'histoire en contradiction avec cette conclusion de notre philosophe. Ouvrons les *Annales* de Tacite, ces fastes de la méchanceté des hommes; parcourons le règne de Tibère, de Claude, de Caligula, de Néron, de Galba, et le destin rapide de tous leurs courtisans; et renonçons à nos principes, si dans la foule de ces scélérats insignes qui déchirèrent les entrailles de leur patrie, et dont les fureurs ont ensanglanté toutes les pages, toutes les lignes de cette histoire, nous rencontrons un heureux....

But then the evidence gradually becomes more specific:

> Les délices de Caprée nous font-elles envier la condition de Tibère? Remontons à l'origine de sa grandeur, suivons sa fortune, considérons-le dans sa retraite, appuyons sur sa fin; et, tout bien examiné, demandons-nous si nous voudrions être à présent ce qu'il fut autrefois, le tyran de son pays, le meurtrier des siens, l'esclave d'une troupe de prostituées, et le protecteur d'une troupe d'esclaves....

Finally, Diderot concentrates his attention upon the case of Nero and Seneca, but he does not content himself with an enumeration of Nero's crimes ("Néron fait perir Britannicus son frère...."); he tries to make us *see* Nero in agony, punished for his evil deeds by his own misery —

> On le *voit* dans d'éternelles horreurs: ses transes vont quelquefois jusqu'à l'aliénation d'esprit; alors il aperçoit le Ténare entr'ouvert, il se croit poursuivi des furies; il ne sait où ni comment échapper à leurs flambeaux vengeurs. (*Essai*, 118 note)

Diderot rarely uses the *passé simple* in this passage: it is the present tense which recreates the scenes of history.

While Diderot may begin a note with a reformulation or expansion of Shaftesbury's point, he will support this statement with particular, concrete *illustration*, with an example, real or imagined. The note below, in which Diderot replaces Shaftesbury's theoretical "timelessness" with immediate reality, is annexed to the following passage of the *Inquiry:*

The parts and proportions of the mind, their mutual relation and dependency, the connection and frame of those passions which constitute the soul or temper, may easily be understood by anyone who thinks it worth his while to study this inward anatomy. 'Tis certain that the order or symmetry of this inward part is in itself no less real and exact than that of the body. However, 'tis apparent that few of us endeavor to become anatomists of this sort. Nor is any one ashamed of the deepest ignorance in such a subject. (283-84)	On se pique de connaître les qualités d'un bon cheval, d'un bon chien, et d'un bon oiseau. On est parfaitement instruit des affections, du tempérament, des humeurs et de la forme convenable à chacune de ces espèces.... *Suivons cet écervelé* qui, pour quelque ordre futile et peut-être déshonnête, différé ou maladroitement exécuté, ferait périr un domestique sous le bâton; *suivons-le* dans ses écuries, et *demandons-lui* pourquoi ce cheval est séparé de la société des autres: "Il a la jambe fine, il porte noblement sa tête, il est en apparence plein d'âme et de feu. — Vous avez raison, vous répondra-t-il.... (*Essai*, 67-68 note)

Having seen evidence of the care Diderot takes to buttress the philosophical argument with particular examples, and, consequently, his recourse to dialogue, both within the text itself of the *Essai* and in the notes, his use of metaphor and descriptive language, his "staging" of a scene from the life of Nero, we should not be surprised to find in the *Essai* signs of Diderot's interest in the theatre. He tells us, for example, in an early note (p. 25) of his own love of the theatre — of the tears he sheds for "les malheurs d'Andromaque" and of the "boutades" of Molière's Alceste. Here the capacity to be deeply moved by tragedy is associated with other characteristics of *l'homme bienfaisant* — and it is to be noted that Diderot, unlike Jean-Jacques, *laughs* at Alceste, whose wish to turn his back on society and withdraw to a *désert* is, we presume, found to be worthy of ridicule. And the best theatre is that which inspires in us admiration for virtue and good deeds:

> Les affections sociales ne montrent toute leur valeur que dans les grandes afflictions. Si ce genre de passions est adroitement remué, comme il arrive à la représentation d'une bonne tragédie, il n'y a aucun plaisir, à égalité de durées, qu'on puisse comparer à ce plaisir d'illusion. Celui qui sait nous intéresser au destin du mérite et de la vertu, nous attendrir sur le sort des bons, et soulever tout ce que nous avons d'humanité, celui-là, dis-je, nous jette dans un ravissement, et nous procure une satisfaction d'esprit et de cœur supérieure à tout ce que les sens ou les appétits causent de plaisirs. (*Essai*, 82) [10]

Even the wonders of God's creation are a *grand spectacle:* "Si nous arrivions dans ce monde avec cette raison que nous portâmes dans la salle de l'Opéra, la première fois que nous y entrâmes, et si la toile se levait brusquement, frappés de la grandeur, de la magnificence et du jeu des décorations, nous n'aurions pas la force

---

[10] The idea is present in Shaftesbury's text; Diderot does not change the sense (see *Inquiry*, 297-98). As far as Diderot is concerned, we are told then long before *De la poésie dramatique* and the *Eloge de Térence* of the poet's function, that the theatre is the meeting-place of *good* people, and that Terence is to be admired for his faithful portrayal of life and manners ("exprimer les sentiments et les mœurs d'un peuple dans sa conduite ordinaire familière, c'est le propre de la comédie, et dans Térence surtout"; *Essai*, 46 note).

de nous refuser à la connaissance de l'ouvrier éternel qui a préparé le spectacle" (*Essai,* 50 note). [11]

That Diderot, in preparing his translation of the *Inquiry,* hoped to render philosophy more *sensible* is clear, for what he says of the *moralistes français* in his *Discours préliminaire* of the *Essai* is reiterated in the *Eloge de Richardson* some fifteen years later:

> Tout ce que Montaigne, Charron, La Rochefoucauld et Nicole ont mis en maximes, Richardson l'a mis en action....
> Une maxime est une règle abstraite et générale de conduite dont on nous laisse l'application à faire. Elle n'imprime par elle-même aucune image sensible dans notre esprit: mais celui qui agit, on le voit, on se met à sa place ou à ses côtés, on se passionne pour ou contre lui; on s'unit à son rôle, s'il est vertueux; on s'en écarte avec indignation, s'il est injuste et vicieux. (*Eloge de Richardson,* in *Œuvres esthétiques,* ed. Vernière, Classiques Garnier, 1959, pp. 29-30)

Richardson's merit lies in the fact that he has done more than *demonstrate* ethical verities: "S'il importe aux hommes d'être persuadés qu'indépendamment de toute considération ultérieure à cette vie, nous n'avons rien de mieux à faire pour être heureux que d'être vertueux, quel service Richardson n'a-t-il pas rendu à l'espèce humaine? *Il n'a point démontré cette vérité; mais il l'a*

---

[11] We have treated this note in greater detail in Chapter I of our study. Diderot takes his inspiration for the opera image and our inability to appreciate the workings of nature from Fontenelle:

> ...Les vrais philosophes passent leur vie à ne point croire ce qu'ils voient, et à tâcher de deviner ce qu'ils ne voient point; et cette condition n'est pas, ce me semble, trop à envier. Sur cela je me figure toujours que la nature est un grand spectacle qui ressemble à celui de l'opéra. Du lieu où vous êtes à l'opéra, vous ne voyez pas le théâtre tout à fait comme il est; on a disposé les décorations et les machines pour faire de loin un effet agréable, et on cache à votre vue ces roues et ces contrepoids qui font tous les mouvements. Aussi ne vous embarassez-vous guère de deviner comment tout cela joue.... Ce qui, à l'égard des philosophes, augmente la difficulté, c'est que dans les machines que la nature présente à nos yeux, les cordes sont parfaitement bien cachées, et elles le sont si bien, qu'on a été longtemps à deviner ce qui causait les mouvements de l'univers. (*Entretiens sur la pluralité des mondes,* "Premier soir")

fait sentir" (*ibid.*, p. 32; my italics). Images are more easily grasped and retained than abstract notions, a point Diderot often makes throughout his work, and his belief that philosophy should not be divorced from *images sensibles* accounts for his wish to render Shaftesbury's "démonstration métaphisique" more concrete, more *real*, just as it in part stimulates his interest in the theatre as a means of teaching moral excellence and in Richardson's novels as moral guides. The "teaching methods" which Diderot describes in the much later *Encyclopédie* article "Leçon" (reprinted in Assézat-Tourneux, XV) have already then been exemplified in his own *Essai sur le mérite et la vertu*:

> En métaphysique, morale, politique, principes des arts, etc. il faut que le fait ou l'exemple suive la leçon, si vous voulez rendre la leçon utile. On formerait mieux la raison en faisant observer la liaison naturelle des choses et des idées qu'en donnant l'habitude de faire des arguments; il faut mêler l'histoire naturelle et civile, la fable, les emblêmes, les allégories, à ce qu'il peut y avoir d'abstrait dans les leçons qu'on donne à la jeunesse; on pourrait imaginer d'exécuter une suite de tableaux dont l'ensemble instruirait des devoirs des citoyens etc. (A.-T., XV, 416-17)

Diderot may have been influenced in his liberal use of dialogue by the style of Shaftesbury's later works, which Diderot probably read at the same time he read the *Inquiry*. Shaftesbury himself was not unaware of the advantages of presenting philosophy in the guise of poetry and drama, and from this point of view he seems to have preferred *The Moralists, A Philosophical Rhapsody, Being a Recital of Certain Conversations on Natural and Moral Subjects* to the *Inquiry*: "So much is our author, by virtue of this piece [*The Moralists*], a poet in due form, and by a more apparent claim than if he had writ a play or dramatic piece in as regular a manner, at least, as any known on our stage," (*Miscellaneous Reflections*, in *Characteristics* II, 333-34). Shaftesbury saw that dialogue is "an improving method," and was used by poets in the effort to ameliorate manners and morals before the philosophers realized its utility (see *Advice to an Author*, in *Characteristics* II, 129-30), and he has recognized that dialogue requires not only a more active participation of the reader (he must judge independently of the author's cajoling), but that it reduces generalities to particular contexts: "You are not only left to judge coolly and with indifference of the sense delivered, but of the character, genius, elocution, and manner of the persons who deliver it.... And for an artist who draws naturally, 'tis not enough to show us merely faces which may be called men's: every face must be a certain man's" (*Advice*, 132).

Perhaps Diderot wished to incorporate some of the "poetic" qualities of *The Moralists* into his translation of the *Inquiry;* in any case, in attempting to render Shaftesbury's argument more personal and more immediately relevant by creating *images* — by inventing dialogue and substituting figurative language for less *picturesque* expression — Diderot is in 1745 already both *philosophe* and *poète*.[12]

---

[12] For further consideration of eighteenth-century French fiction as "moral exercise," see Vivienne Mylne, *The Eighteenth-Century French Novel: Techniques of Illusion*, Manchester University Press, 1965, Chapter I.

CONCLUSION

I hope that the present study has served to dispel some of the notions about the *Essai sur le mérite et la vertu* which have been formed and perpetuated in neglect. The translation itself, even apart from the accompanying footnotes, far from being a perfunctory rendering of Shaftesbury's *Inquiry*, allows us much insight into the state of Diderot's development a year before the appearance of the *Pensées philosophiques*, two years previous to the writing of *La Promenade du sceptique*,[1] and four years prior to the publication of the *Lettre sur les aveugles*. A great distance separates the Diderot of the *Essai* from Diderot author of the *Lettre sur les aveugles*, but the distance is not so vast as we have been led to believe by those who claim that Diderot's rendering of the *Inquiry* indicates his unqualified sympathy with Shaftesbury's philoosphy. To be sure, Diderot was attracted to the writings of the English deist because, as he himself suggests, Shaftesbury's thinking offers an antidote to metaphysics and an attempt to formulate an ethic based on experience. It is clear that Diderot saw a kindred spirit in Shaftesbury, with the latter's anti-clerical bias, his scorn of "enthusiasm" and superstition *and* nihilistic skepticism, his belief in intuitively perceived ethical and esthetic standards, and his effort to prove that virtuous conduct is the surest means to the achievement of happiness. Evidently, Diderot is not yet an atheist in 1745, nor even so receptive to skepticism as the *Pensées philosophiques* of 1746 indicate, but the

---

[1] Since we do not know the exact date of the composition of *La Promenade du sceptique*, I should say here that the *Essai* was *probably* composed before a final redaction of what was to become *La Promenade du sceptique*.

Essai is a document of transition. Signs there are in the *Essai* of a faith that is wavering and a spirit that is questioning the religious explanation of things: we have seen his impatience with the hypothesis of an all-encompassing natural and moral order and with religious institutions, and we have noted his various attempts to show not only the independence of ethics from religious belief, but that objective moral and esthetic values exist free from the context of any supernatural creating principle.

Diderot already in 1745 possesses the intellectual and polemical equipment of the *philosophes* in his knowledge of and borrowing from Cicero, Petronius, Lucretius (who will of course greatly influence his materialism), and Tacitus, Montaigne, Locke, and Swift, and if we are not taken aback by his attacks on the scholastic tradition, religious dogma, and the celibacy of the clergy, it is because the choice of these targets reflects after all the spirit of his time and of the *Inquiry* — even though Diderot often belabors his adversaries with greater vigor than Shaftesbury does in the *Inquiry* itself. Let it no longer be said however, that Diderot "tones down" the audacity of Shaftesbury. Aside from Diderot's insistence in his *Discours préliminaire* upon the distinction between deism and theism (which, as we have shown, is a specious one, invented for the sake of subterfuge), it is Diderot, not Shaftesbury, who gives the *Essai* any subversive character it may possess. What Diderot hesitates to do even in his later most overtly atheistic works he feels secure in doing beneath the cover of a "translation" and in the guise of an English author: he presents a surprisingly militant stance against the injustices of contemporary *political* institutions.

Diderot did not suddenly acquire independence with the composition and publication of the *Pensées philosophiques;* indeed, the resemblances of form and content between the *Essai* and the *Pensées philosophiques* (again, Diderot's footnotes to the *Essai* can be seen as "pensées philosophiques") in the fragmentary nature of the 1746 work and what it owes in inspiration and content to Diderot's experience of translating the *Inquiry,* are apparent. The *Essai sur le mérite et la vertu* should be recognized in its own right as the product of a good deal of *self*-assertion on Diderot's part.

SELECTED BIBLIOGRAPHY

As I have indicated in a note to my preface, the primary sources for this study are Diderot's *Essai sur le mérite et la vertu* in *Œuvres complètes*, I, ed. Assézat and Tourneux, Paris, 1876, and Shaftesbury's *An Inquiry Concerning Virtue or Merit*, in *The Characteristics*, ed. J. M. Robertson, London, 1900. I list below only those critical studies which I have found to be particularly relevant to Diderot's *Essai*, either in terms of the translation or with respect to certain concepts and problems with which one must deal in an assessment of the text.

CASINI, PAOLO. "Diderot e Shaftesbury," *Giornale critico della filosofia italiana*, XXXIX (XIV), 1960, 250-269.
——. *Diderot "Philosophe."* Bari, 1962.
CROCKER, LESTER. *Two Diderot Studies: Ethics and Esthetics*. Baltimore, 1952.
CRU, R. L. *Diderot and English Thought*. New York, 1913.
DIECKMANN, HERBERT. *Cinq Leçons sur Diderot*. Geneva and Paris, 1959.
FOLKIERSKI, WLADISLAW. "L'Anglais de Diderot," *Revue de Littérature comparée*, April-June 1960, 226-244.
HERMAND, PIERRE. *Les Idées morales de Diderot*. Paris, 1923.
LEGROS, RENÉ. "Diderot et Shaftesbury," *Modern Language Review*, XIX, 1924, 188-194.
LEWINTER, ROGER. "L'Exaltation de la vertu dans le théâtre de Diderot," *Diderot Studies VIII*, Geneva, 1966, 119-169.
LÖPELMANN, MARTIN. *Der Junge Diderot*. Berlin, 1934.
POMMIER, JEAN. *Diderot avant Vincennes*. Paris, 1939.
ROGER, JACQUES. "Le Déisme du jeune Diderot," *Europäische Aufklärung: Herbert Dieckman zum 60. Geburtstag*, ed. Friedrich and Schalk. Munich, 1967.
SCHLEGEL, DOROTHY. *Shaftesbury and The French Deists*. Chapel Hill, North Carolina, 1956.
THIELEMANN, LELAND. "Diderot and Hobbes," *Diderot Studies II*, Geneva, 1952, 221-278.
VARTANIAN, ARAM. "From Deist to Atheist: Diderot's Philosophical Orientation, 1746-1749," *Diderot Studies I*, Syracuse, New York, 1949.
VENTURI, FRANCO. *La Jeunesse de Diderot*. Paris, 1939.
WILSON, ARTHUR M. *Diderot: The Testing Years, 1713-1759*. New York, 1959.

www.ingramcontent.com/pod-product-compliance
Lightning Source LLC
Chambersburg PA
CBHW020420230426
43663CB00007BA/1255